THE WILDER MUIR

THE WILDER MUIR

The Curious Nature of John Muir

EDITED AND INTRODUCED BY
BONNIE J. GISEL

ILLUSTRATIONS BY
FIONA KING

YOSEMITE CONSERVANCY
Yosemite National Park

Throughout *The Wilder Muir*, many of John Muir's original spellings and place names have been preserved to accurately portray his writings; however, some spellings have been modernized so as not to appear as errors. Numerals have been revised per *The Chicago Manual of Style* and most of the punctuation has been updated to aid the reader. On occasion, a brief note accompanies an original term for additional clarification.

YOSEMITE
CONSERVANCY.

yosemiteconservancy.org

Yosemite Conservancy inspires people to support projects and programs that preserve Yosemite and enrich the visitor experience.

Library of Congress Control Number: 2016962405

Cover art by Fiona King
Design by Nancy Austin

ISBN 978-1-930238-75-6
Printed in the USA by McNaughton & Gunn
Manufactured using recycled paper

1 2 3 4 5 6 – 21 20 19 18 17

FSC
www.fsc.org
MIX
Paper from
responsible sources
FSC® C011935

For Nikolaus

CONTENTS

CONTENTS

INTRODUCTION

John Muir was born in 1838 on High Street in Dunbar, Scotland. As a boy, he was fond of his parents' garden, cultivated as a source of family pride, surrounded by a high wall banked with boxwood hedges. Fond of all things wild, John and his brother David would often pull themselves over the garden wall and play along the shore of Belhaven Bay. Urged on by spiritual fervor, John's father, David, immigrated to the United States in the spring of 1849 to join the Disciples of Christ. Three of the Muir children (Sarah, John, and David) initially accompanied their father to south-central Wisconsin. John's mother, Ann G. Muir, and the remaining children (Margaret, Daniel, and the twins, Mary and Annie) would arrive that fall. Joanna, John's youngest sister, was born in Wisconsin. The Muir family settled near Portage on the Fox River, on a parcel of 160 acres of open woodland where they built a bur-oak shanty. They constructed a two-story, eight-room house, which they named Fountain Lake Farm. John's sympathy, respect, love, and affection for animals were nurtured throughout his boyhood on the farm. Animals, he later wrote, are our "earth-born companions."[1]

Fountain Lake Farm was the source of income for the Muir family, and the Muir children bore the brunt of the toil, cultivating and harvesting the crops. In their free time in the evenings and on Sundays, John and his brothers drifted on Fountain Lake in a boat John built from pine boards. For eight years the family lived at Fountain Lake. The purchase of fertile land four miles southeast of the farm meant that John, then seventeen, walked from Fountain Lake to Hickory Hill for two growing seasons until a T-shaped two-story house was built there. With what little time remained after farm work was done, John studied mathematics, history, natural history, philosophy, and the life of noted naturalist and explorer Alexander von Humboldt. At Hickory Hill, John would often retreat to the stone-walled cellar early in the morning. Too cold to read, he would carve inventions in wood: a four-foot-long model of a self-setting sawmill, water-wheels, door locks and latches, thermometers, hygrometers, pyrometers, barometers, clocks, an automatic contrivance for feeding horses, a lamp-lighter, fire-lighter, and an early-rising bed.

In the fall of 1860, John Muir, then twenty-two, left Portage. At the Wisconsin State Agricultural Society Fair, he exhibited his wooden inventions—a set of clocks and a thermometer—for which he received a diploma and five dollars. His early-rising bed, installed on the fairground, raised its occupants to an upright position with feet upon the footboard. The bed drew a receptive audience, including Jeanne Carr. She was responsible for reporting to fair officials on Muir's award-winning inventions. Her introduction to Muir at the fair may have been forgotten if her husband, Dr. Ezra S. Carr, professor of chemistry and natural history at the University of Wisconsin at Madison, had not reported to her Muir's attendance in his lectures in geology the following year. Dr. James D. Butler, professor of classics, encouraged Muir to keep a daily journal while studying at the university. Milton Griswold, a fellow student, introduced Muir to the study of botany. The Carrs invited Muir to their home to study in their library, and at some point offered him a room (which he declined). By the time Muir left the university in 1863, he and the Carrs had become close friends. When Muir departed Madison in early 1864, having spent five semesters at the university and three summers collecting plant specimens, he took with him a genuine aptitude for recording his experiences and discoveries in a journal, a commitment to the study of botany, and his friendship with the Carrs. In search of beauty and knowledge, Muir headed east by train to Winsor, Canada, to study plants. A letter from Jeanne Carr reached him at the Trout sawmill near Meaford, Canada, where he was manufacturing wooden rakes and broom handles. Encouraged to exchange thoughts, Muir penned a letter to her in September 1865 that began a thirty-year correspondence.[2]

Muir traveled from Canada to Indianapolis to the Gulf of Mexico and arrived in California in 1868. The letters he wrote to Jeanne Carr revealed ideas and feelings he had not shared with other family members or friends. She recognized his unique gift for writing, and her reassuring and inspiring letters encouraged Muir to write for publication. The Carrs moved to Oakland, California, in late 1868. The following year, Ezra S. Carr joined the faculty at the University of California, where he taught horticulture, agriculture, and chemistry. Muir rejoiced in their move, and their proximity provided the opportunity for Jeanne to introduce him to friends and acquaintances, among them Ralph Waldo Emerson. Muir began to apply himself to the publication of his observations of the natural world. He wrote letters and kept a journal, edited both into manuscripts, and ultimately published them as articles. In an 1874 letter to Jeanne, Muir clarified his purpose: he "cared to live only to entice people to look at Nature's loveliness." His storytelling and writing became the means to accomplish this goal.[3]

Muir would spend his life sauntering through as much of the natural world as he was able, searching for answers to the unsolved questions that lay before him. Recognizing he was no ordinary person, as he set out on his journey, he described himself as ebbing and flooding beyond boundaries, determined to invent himself as he went along. In appearance to family and friends, Muir engendered "a spiritual insight into Nature's lore granted only to those who love and woo her in her great outdoor palaces." A man engaged in process, on a mission "doomed," he wrote, "to be carried by the spirit into the wilderness," Muir was swept onward in a general current that bore on irresistibly.[4]

What is it about John Muir that ignites in us something so powerful and endearing? We are drawn to savor his journey. Some stories seem beyond the scope of human endurance; and others are subtle and sublime in close observation. Though Muir found writing to be arduous, we find his writings fluid, accessible, and visionary. We recognize that his intended purpose was to breathe life into the human imagination about the natural world. Through Muir's writings we gain a deeper understanding of the value he placed on nature, and we in turn are inspired. His poetic prose, after years of empirical study, became the voice of wilderness and its preservation.

The Wilder Muir presents twenty-three tales of Muir's wild and curious wanderings, selected from letters, journals, articles, and books. They are presented in the order the events occurred. Often in Muir's writings he appears alone or he wrote of his adventures as if he had been alone. In many of these selections he includes family, friends, and colleagues. While Muir's published work is primarily a compendium of his exploration and observations of California and Alaska, here we first encounter him with the *Calypso borealis* in Canada in 1864. Next we find him sleeping on a grave in Bonaventure Cemetery in Savannah, Georgia, in 1867, having walked over landscapes and among trees he had never before seen. Muir decided to go to California. Upon arriving in San Francisco, he and a fellow traveler, a young Englishman nearly his age by the name of Chilwell who agreed to tramp with him, hiked to Yosemite Valley in the spring of 1868. Muir found the magnitude of the mountains remarkable. Convinced that the Sierra Nevada required a good long time to study, he found employment in California where, between 1870 and 1873, friendships were nurtured, his empirical studies exploded, and his professional writing career began. Muir met scientists, philosophers, academics, artists, and writers, many of whom were introduced to him by Jeanne Carr. To these colleagues he turned for support over the years.

Following journeys that began in 1871 into the Tuolumne Canyon, upon living glaciers, into the southern Sierra, and trekking up Mount Shasta, Mount Whitney, and Half Dome, a wistful Muir bathed in Utah's Great Salt Lake in 1877. After introducing the water ouzel, he traveled to Lake Tahoe in 1878 and boarded the *Corwin* in 1881, where he visited Herald Island in the Arctic Ocean. A return trip to Yosemite Valley in 1884, this time with his wife, Louie Wanda Strentzel Muir, would be her first and last trip away from their Alhambra Valley, California, home. An excursion to Mount Rainier in 1887 with a group of climbers provides insight into the horror of outdated food and the dangers of trekking. Muir undertook a second trip into the Grand Canyon of the Tuolumne in 1895 cautiously hiking, discarding most of what he carried, including his food and his drinking cup. While California remained Muir's home, he traveled to Alaska and the Arctic, across the United States and to Europe, Egypt, India, Russia, China, Japan, the Philippines, Australia, New Zealand, Hawaii, South America, and Africa, searching for indigenous trees about which he had studied and visiting botanical gardens. In Chile, Muir's quest for the *Araucaria imbricata* (the monkey puzzle tree) in 1911, led him to near snowline in the Andes.

Few of us are able to reach the destinations Muir did; even fewer are endowed with his keen observational skills. But through his ability to record with clarity the natural world he experienced, Muir helps us to see the world so precious to him. Here, between the *Calypso borealis* and the *Araucaria imbricata*, are adventures where friendships and family germinated and were incorporated and purposed toward a greater and growing awareness of wilderness and the preservation of the natural world. These selections of Muir's writings allow us to follow his trek into the mountains and wild places. In turn, we find there more than we seek.

Bonnie J. Gisel
Yosemite National Park
February 1, 2017

THE ADVENTURES

CALYPSO BOREALIS

L EAVING PORTAGE, WISCONSIN, with the first signs of spring in March 1864, twenty-five-year-old John Muir traveled by train to Winsor, Canada. He may have boarded the Great Western Railway barreling into southern Ontario. His journal of 1864 is missing, so his first six months in Canada remain somewhat unclear. However, Muir wrote letters to family and friends and collected plant specimens with note-billets from which locations, if not details, may be determined.

John Muir met his brother Daniel at Niagara Falls, and together they returned to Meaford, located on Nottawasaga Bay, a sub-basin of Georgian Bay and Owen Sound Bay, where Daniel had been working at a mill and factory owned by William H. Trout and Charles Jay. Daniel returned to the United States in May 1865. John remained at the factory, making improvements to the machinery that produced rake and broom handles and set rake teeth. On Sundays he studied botany. He took a leave from the mill and traveled to Owen Sound, about nineteen miles from Meaford, on an extended plant-collecting expedition in search of the *Calypso borealis*.

Only once in 1864 did Muir find what he considered the rarest and most beautiful plant: the *Calypso borealis,* known as "the lady slipper orchid." In March 1866, the letter he wrote to Jeanne Carr in which he described his encounter with the *Calypso borealis* was taken from the Carr home by Dr. James D. Butler, with whom Muir had studied at the University of Wisconsin. Butler copied and published the letter in the *Boston Recorder* in December 1866. Unbeknownst to Muir, the story of the perfectly spiritual plant initiated his writing career. In later years Muir recalled the two significant moments in his life were the discovery of the *Calypso borealis* and meeting Ralph Waldo Emerson in 1871.[1]

* * *

INTRODUCTION BY DR. JAMES D. BUTLER

A young Wisconsin gatherer of simples seems not a whit behind Thoreau as a scrutinizer and votary of nature. During the last season but one, he explored the flora of Canada—playing the pedestrian from Lake Superior to Niagara, setting out with primroses which come before the swallow dares, and take the winds of March with beauty, nor tiring till black fronts hid the last of the flowers.

He [Muir] writes:

I did find *Calypso*—but only once, far in the depths of the very wildest of Canadian dark woods, near those high, cold, moss-covered swamps where most of the peninsular streams of Canada West take their rise.

For several days in June, I had been forcing my way through woods that seemed to become more and more dense, and among bogs more and more difficult to cross, when, one warm afternoon, after descending a hillside covered with huge half-dead hemlocks, I crossed an ice-cold stream, and espied two specimens of *Calypso*. There, upon an open plat of yellow moss, near an immense rotten log, were these little plants, so pure.

They were alone. Not a vine was near, not a blade of grass, nor a bush. Nor were there any birds or insects, for great blocks of ice lay screened from the summer's sun by deep beds of moss, and chilled the water. They were indeed alone, for the dull, ignoble hemlocks were not companions, nor was the nearer arbor-vitae, with its root-like, pendulous branches decaying confusedly on the wet, cold ground.

I never before saw a plant so full of life; so perfectly spiritual, it seemed pure enough for the throne of its Creator. I felt as if I were in the presence of superior beings who loved me and beckoned me to come. I sat down beside them and wept for joy. Could angels in their better land show us a more beautiful plant? How good is our Heavenly Father in granting us such friends as are these plant-creatures, filling us wherever we go with pleasure so deep, so pure, so endless.

I cannot understand the nature of the curse, "Thorns and thistles shall it bring forth to thee." Is our world indeed the worse for this "thistly curse?" Are not all plants beautiful? Or in some way useful? Would not the world suffer by the banishment of a single weed? The curse must be within ourselves.

Excerpt from "For the *Boston Recorder*. The *Calypso Borealis*. Botanical Enthusiasm. From Prof. J. D. Butler," *Boston Recorder* (December 21, 1866): 1.

BONAVENTURE CEMETERY

A FIRE IN FEBRUARY 1866 destroyed Trout's mill in Meaford, Canada. Within a month, John Muir left for the industrial center of Indianapolis, where he found work at Osgood & Smith, a wholesale manufacturer of hubs, spokes, and broom and rake handles. Indianapolis was surrounded by a rich forest of deciduous trees, and on Sundays he walked out beyond the city into the forest to collect plants. By January 1867, Muir was studying maps and planning an extended botanical excursion through the southern United States. On March 5, as he replaced a countershaft for a circular saw, the belt stretched. Muir laced it with a pointed file, which slipped and pierced his right eye at the edge of the cornea. Half-blind, in a darkened room for weeks, he thought about plants he would never see. The injury precipitated Muir's departure from Indianapolis. For fear of any further affliction that would render him incapable of seeing, he was driven to store his mind with as much natural beauty as he could. Slowly his sight returned, and although his vision would never be

perfect, Muir bade adieu to mechanical inventions, determined to devote his life to the study of the natural world. He
set out to travel south on a thousand-mile walk to the Gulf
of Mexico to study the "vegetation of the warm end of the
country."[1]

Doomed, he believed, to be carried into the wilderness,
and uncertain as to what exactly drove him, Muir no doubt
had been influenced by the study of geology at the University of Wisconsin with Dr. Ezra S. Carr and by his affection
for plants and for the study of botany. Muir recognized the
world as an open book for him to explore, puzzle over, and
enjoy. On the first day of September, Muir, now twenty-nine,
traveled from Indianapolis to Kentucky. In the outskirts of
Louisville he opened a map and planned his trip. Pushing on
in a southward direction, he carried a small satchel, a book
of Robert Burns's poems, Milton's *Paradise Lost,* a copy of
the New Testament, and a plant press. In Tennessee, Muir
ascended the Cumberland Mountains, the first mountains he
ever climbed, and as he crossed the Clinch River, he began to
notice plants and trees he did not recognize.

Continuing southward, Muir arrived in Athens, Georgia. Strange plants crowded around him, and there were
few familiar faces among all the flowers in a day's walk.
Near Augusta he reached the northern limit of the southern
yellow pine and marveled at the cypress swamps. Reaching
Savannah nearly penniless, Muir waited for money to arrive
from his brother David, who lived in Portage, Wisconsin. He

found a white-shelled road that led four miles from Savannah to the Bonaventure Cemetery. The glory of Bonaventure
was its noble avenue of live oaks draped in Tillandsia moss.
Hanging in long silvery-gray skeins, the moss reached toward
the ground and slowly waved in the wind. Everything that
grew gained Muir's attention, and he planned to become
acquainted with as many plants as he could.

* * *

I had only about a dollar and a half left in my purse, and so was compelled
to camp out to make it last in buying only bread. I went out of the noisy
town to seek a sleeping place that was not marshy. After gaining the outskirts of the town toward the sea, I found some low sand dunes, yellow with
flowering solidagoes.

I wandered wearily from dune to dune, sinking ankle-deep in the
sand, searching for a place to sleep beneath the tall flowers, free from insects
and snakes. . . . The wind had strange sounds, waving the heavy panicles
over my head, and I feared sickness from malaria so prevalent here, when I
suddenly thought of the graveyard.

"There," thought I, "is an ideal place for a penniless wanderer. There,
no superstitious, prowling mischief-maker dares venture for fear of haunting
ghosts; while for me, there will be God's rest and peace. And then, if I am to
be exposed to unhealthy vapors, I shall have capital compensation in seeing
those grand oaks in the moonlight, with all the impressive and nameless
influences of this lonely beautiful place." [2]

By this time it was near sunset, and I hastened across the common to the road and set off for Bonaventure, delighted with my choice, and almost glad to find that necessity had furnished me with so good an excuse for doing what I knew my mother would censure; for she made me promise I would not lie out of doors if I could possibly avoid it. . . . I arrived near the graves in the silent hour of the gloaming.

I was very thirsty after walking so long in the muggy heat, a distance of three or four miles from the city, to get to this graveyard. A dull, sluggish, coffee-colored stream flows under the road just outside the graveyard garden park, from which I managed to get a drink after breaking a way down to the water through a dense fringe of bushes, daring the snakes and alligators in the dark. Thus refreshed, I entered the weird and beautiful abode of the dead.

All the avenue where I walked was in shadow, but an exposed tombstone frequently shone out in startling whiteness on either hand, and thickets of sparkleberry bushes gleamed like heaps of crystal. Not a breath of air moved the gray moss, and the great black arms of the trees met overhead and covered the avenue. But the canopy was fissured by many a netted seam and leafy-edged opening, through which the moonlight sifted in auroral rays, broidering the blackness in silvery light. Though tired, I sauntered a while enchanted, then lay down under one of the great oaks. I found a little mound that served for a pillow, placed my plant press and bag beside me and rested fairly well, though somewhat disturbed by large prickly-footed beetles creeping across my hands and face, and by a lot of hungry, stinging mosquitoes.

When I awoke, the sun was up and all Nature was rejoicing. Some birds had discovered me as an intruder and were making a great ado in interesting language and gestures. I heard the screaming of the bald eagles. . . . On rising, I found that my head had been resting on a grave, and though my sleep had not been quite so sound as that of the person below, I arose refreshed, and looking about me, the morning sunbeams pouring through the oaks and gardens dripping with dew, the beauty displayed was so glorious and exhilarating that hunger and care seemed only a dream.

Eating a breakfast cracker or two and watching for a few hours the beautiful light, birds, squirrels, and insects, I returned to Savannah, to find my money package had not yet arrived. I then decided to go early to the graveyard and make a nest with a roof to keep off the dew, as there was no way of finding out how long I might have to stay. I chose a hidden spot in a dense thicket of sparkleberry bushes, near the right bank of the Savannah River, where the bald eagles and a multitude of singing birds roosted. It was so well hidden that I had to carefully fix its compass bearing in my mind from a mark I made on the side of the main avenue, that I might be able to find it at bedtime.

I used four of the bushes as corner posts for my little hut, which was about four or five feet long by about three or four in width, tied little branches across from forks in the bushes to support a roof of rushes, and spread a thick mattress of long moss over the floor for a bed. My whole establishment was on so small a scale that I could have taken up, not only my bed, but my whole house, and walked. There I lay that night, eating a few crackers.

Next day I returned to the town and was disappointed as usual in obtaining money. So after spending the day looking at the plants in the gardens of the fine residences and town squares, I returned to my graveyard home. That I might not be observed and suspected of hiding, as if I had committed a crime, I always went home after dark, and one night, as I lay down in my moss nest, I felt some cold-blooded creature in it; whether a snake or simply a frog or toad, I do not know, but instinctively, instead of drawing back my hand, I grasped the poor creature and threw it over the tops of the bushes. That was the only significant disturbance or fright that I got.

In the morning everything seemed divine. Only squirrels, sunbeams, and birds came about me. I was awakened every morning by these little singers after they discovered my nest. Instead of serenely singing their morning songs, they at first came within two or three feet of the hut, and looking in at me through the leaves, chattered and scolded in half-angry, half-wondering tones. The crowd constantly increased, attracted by the disturbance. Thus I began to get acquainted with my bird neighbors in this blessed wilderness, and after they learned that I meant them no ill, they scolded less and sang more.

After five days of this graveyard life I saw that even with living on three or four cents a day my last twenty-five cents would soon be spent, and after trying again and again unsuccessfully to find some employment, began to think that I must strike farther out into the country, but still within reach of town, until I came to some grain or rice field that had not yet been harvested, trusting that I could live indefinitely on toasted or raw corn or rice.

By this time I was becoming faint, and in making the journey to the town was alarmed to find myself growing staggery and giddy. The ground ahead seemed to be rising up in front of me, and the little streams in the ditches on the sides of the road seemed to be flowing uphill. Then I realized that I was becoming dangerously hungry and became more than ever anxious to receive that money package.

To my delight this fifth or sixth morning, when I inquired if the money package had come, the clerk replied that it had.

Excerpt from John Muir, *A Thousand-Mile Walk to the Gulf* (Boston: Houghton Mifflin, 1916), 72–79.

FIRST TRIP TO YOSEMITE

M ONEY ARRIVED FOR JOHN MUIR in Savannah, and
he booked passage on the steamer *Sylvan Shore* to
north Florida, a half-day's sail. At the town of Fernandina,
he sent plant specimens to his brother David to deliver to
their sister Sarah for safe keeping. In late October 1867,
upon reaching the ocean at Cedar Keys, Muir worked at a
sawmill. An onset of malaria required he convalesce, and
in mid-December he wrote to David that he was a pris-
oner of sickness and often insensible. Still weak with fever,
Muir gathered his plant specimens, boarded the *Island Belle,*
and sailed for Cuba. Wandering among coconut palms, he
climbed aboard the ship each night with a handful of flowers. In Havana, Muir boarded a schooner carrying a cargo of
oranges bound for New York, where he boarded the *Santiago
de Cuba* for Panama. Within little more than a year after leaving Indianapolis, Muir traveled on to California on the steamship *Nebraska*, arriving in San Francisco on April 1, 1868.[1]

Muir and Chilwell, a young Englishman he had met
on the steamship *Nebraska*, crossed from San Francisco to

Oakland on a ferry and boarded a train to East Oakland. On foot, they took the first road they came to, proceeded to San Jose, and turned in an easterly direction toward Yosemite, about which Muir had read in 1866. Crossing immeasurable fields of flowers, then the San Joaquin River, at Hill's Ferry they followed the Merced River into Snelling. From Coulterville, Mariposa County, twenty miles northwest of Mariposa, at an elevation of 1,699 feet, Muir and Chilwell continued east. Reaching Crane Flat, they began their descent into Yosemite Valley. Ten days were spent collecting plants, sketching, and exploring before returning to Snelling by way of Clark's Station and the Mariposa Grove of Big Trees (giant sequoias).[2]

* * *

On the second day of April, 1868, I left San Francisco for Yosemite Valley, companioned by a young Englishman. Our orthodox route of "nearest and quickest" was by steam to Stockton, thence by stage to Coulterville or Mariposa, and the remainder of the way over the mountains on horseback. But we had plenty of time and proposed drifting leisurely mountainward, via the valley of San Jose, Pacheco Pass, and the plain of San Joaquin, and thence to Yosemite by any road that we chanced to find, enjoying the flowers and light, "camping out" in our blankets wherever overtaken by night, and paying very little compliance to roads or times. Accordingly, we crossed "the Bay" by the Oakland ferry, and proceeded up the valley of San Jose.

This is one of the most fertile, of the many small valleys of the coast; its rich bottoms are filled with wheat-fields and orchards and vineyards, and alfalfa meadows. It was now spring-time, and the weather was the best that we ever enjoyed. Larks and streams sang everywhere; the sky was cloudless, and the whole valley was a lake of light. The atmosphere was spicy and exhilarating; my companion acknowledging over his national prejudices that it was the best he ever breathed,—more deliciously fragrant than the hawthorn hedges of England. This San Jose sky was not simply pure and bright and mixed with plenty of well-tempered sunshine, but it possessed a positive flavor—a *taste*—that thrilled from the lungs throughout every tissue of the body; every inspiration yielded a corresponding well-defined piece of pleasure that awakened thousands of new palates everywhere. Both my companion and myself had lived and dozed on common air for nearly thirty years, and never before this discovered that our bodies contained such multitudes of palates, or that this mortal flesh, so little valued by philosophers and teachers, was possessed of so vast a capacity for happiness.

We emerged from this ether baptism new creatures, born again; and truly not until this time were we fairly conscious that we were born at all. Never more, thought I, as we strode forward at faster speed, never more shall I sentimentalize about getting out of the mortal coil: this flesh is not a coil; it is a sponge steeped in immortality.

The foothills (that form the sides of our blessed font) are in near view all the way to Gilroy: those of the Monte Diablo range on our left, those of Santa Cruz on our right; they are smooth and flowing, and come down to the bottom levels in curves of most surpassing beauty; they still wear natural flowers, which do not occur singly or in handfuls, scattered about in the grass, but they grow close together in smooth, cloud-shaped companies, acres and hillsides in size, white, purple, and yellow, separate, yet blending to each other like the hills upon which they grow....The prevailing northwest wind has permanently swayed all unsheltered trees up the valley; groves upon the more exposed hillsides lean forward like patches of lodged wheat. The Santa Cruz Mountains have grand forests of redwood (*Sequoia semper-virens*), some specimens near fifty feet in circumference.

The Pacheco Pass was scarcely less enchanting than the valley. It resounded with crystal waters and the loud shouts of thousands of California quails.

Through a considerable portion of the pass, the road bends and mazes along the groves of a stream or down in its pebbly bed, leading one now deep in the shadows of dogwoods and alders, then out in the light, through dry chaparral, over green carex meadows banked with violets and ferns, and dry, plantless flood-beds of gravel and sand.

In this rich garden pass, we gathered many fine grasses and carices, and brilliant pentstemons, azure and scarlet, and mints and lilies, and scores of others, strangers to us, but beautiful and pure as ever enjoyed the sun or shade of a mountain home.

After we were fairly over the summit of the pass and had reached an open hill-brow, a scene of peerless grandeur burst suddenly upon us. At our feet, basking in sungold, lay the Great Central Plain of California, bounded by the mountains on which we stood, and by the lofty, snow-capped Sierra Nevada; all in grandest simplicity, clear and bright as a new outspread map.

In half a day we were down over all the foothills, past the San Luis Gonzaga Ranch, and wading out in the grand, level ocean of flowers. This plain, watered by the San Joaquin and Sacramento rivers, formed one flower bed, nearly four hundred miles in length by thirty in width.

In this botanist's better land, I drifted separate many days, the largest days of my life, resting at times from the blessed plants, in showers of bugs and sun-born butterflies; or I watched the smooth-bounding antelopes or startled hares, skimming light and swift as eagles' shadows; or, turning from all this fervid life, contemplated the Sierras, that mighty wall up-rising from the brink of this lake of gold, miles in the higher blue, bearing aloft its domes and spires in spotless white, unshining and beamless, yet pure as pearl, clear and undimmed as the flowers at my feet. Never were mortal eyes more thronged with beauty. When I walked, more than a hundred flowers touched my feet, at every step closing above them, as if wading in water. Go where I would, east or west, north or south, I still plashed and rippled in flower-gems; and at night I lay between two skies of silver and gold, spanned by a milky-way, and nestling deep in a goldy-way of vegetable suns.

February and March is the ripe springtime of the plain, April the summer, and May the autumn. The first beginnings of spring are controlled by the rains, which generally appear in December. Rains between May and December are very rare. This is the winter—a winter of drouth and heat. But in no part of the year is plant-life wholly awanting. A few lilies with bulbs very deep in the soil, and a rosy compound called tar-weed, and a species of erigonum, are slender, inconspicuous links which continue the floral chain from season to season around the year.

Ere we were ready to recommence our march to Yosemite, May was about half done. The flowers and grasses, so late in the pomp and power of full bloom, were dead, and their parched leaves crisped and crackled beneath our feet, as if they had literally been "cast into the oven."

After travelling two days among the delightful death of this sunny winter, we came to another summer in the Sierra foothills. Flowers were spread confidingly open, and streams and winds were cool. Above Coulter-ville, forty or fifty miles farther in the mountains, we came to spring. The leaves of the mountain oaks were small and drooping, and still wore their first tintings of crimson and purple; and the wrinkles of their bud-folds were still distinct, as if newly opened; and, scattered over banks and sunny slopes, thousands of gentle plants were tasting life for the first time. A few miles farther, on the Pilot Peak ridge, we came to the edge of a winter. Few growing leaves were to be seen; the highest and youngest of the lilies and spring violets were far below; winter scales were still wrapped close on the buds of dwarf oaks and hazels. The great sugar pines waved their long arms, as if about to speak; and we soon were in deep snow. After we had reached the highest part of the ridge, clouds began to gather, storm winds swept the forest, and snow began to fall thick and blinding. Fortunately, we reached a sort of shingle cabin at Crane Flat, where we sheltered until the next day. Thus, in less than a week from the hot autumn of San Joaquin, we were struggling in a bewildering storm of mountain winter. This was on or about May 20, at an elevation of 6,130 feet. Here the forest is magnificent, composed in part of the sugar pine (*Pinus lambertiana*), which is the king of all pines, most noble in manners and language. Many specimens are over two hundred feet in height, and eight to ten in diameter, fresh and sound as the sun which made them. The yellow pine (*Pinus ponderosa*) also grows here and the cedar (*Libocedrus decurrens*); but the bulk of the forest is made up of the two silver firs (*Picea grandis* and *Picea amabilis*), the former always greatly predominating at this altitude. Descending from this winter towards the Merced, the snow gradually disappeared from the ground and sky, tender leaves unfolded less and less doubtfully, violets and lilies shone about us once more, and at length, arriving in the glorious Yosemite, we found it full of summer and spring. Thus, as colors blend in a rainbow and as mountains curve to a plain, so meet and blend the plants and seasons of this delightsome land.

Excerpt from John Muir, "Rambles of a Botanist Among the Plants and Climates of California," *Old and New* 5 (June 1872): 767–72.

AN ARMY MUSKET

WILLIAM FREDERIC BADÈ, John Muir's literary executor, published Muir's journal account of his first trip into Yosemite Valley with Chilwell, whom Muir found amusing. Nearly the same age as Muir, though Chilwell lacked experience and expressed fear of encountering a bear, he embraced the opportunity to visit Yosemite. Drifting leisurely toward the mountains, they stopped in Coulterville to purchase flour, tea, an old army musket, and a few pounds of quail shot and large buckshot. The winter had been severe, and in some places the trail was still buried in snow eight- to ten-feet deep. Muir was delighted with the thought of ten feet of snow and assured Chilwell that he never got lost.

* * *

JOURNAL ENTRY, 1868

Our bill of fare in camps was simple—tea and cakes, the latter made from flour without leaven and toasted on the coals—and of course we shunned hotels in the valley, seldom indulging even in crackers, as being too expensive. Chilwell, being an Englishman, loudly lamented being compelled to live on so light a diet, flour and water, as he expressed it, and hungered for flesh; therefore, he made desperate efforts to shoot something to eat, particularly quails and grouse, but he was invariably unsuccessful and declared the gun was worthless. I told him I thought that it was good enough if properly loaded and aimed, though perhaps sighted too high, and promised to show him at the first opportunity how to load and shoot.

At Deer Flat the wagon road ended in a trail which we traced up the side of the dividing ridge parallel to the Merced and Tuolumne to Crane Flat, lying at a height of six thousand feet. . . . Here, too, we got into the heavy winter snow—a fine change from the burning foothills and plains.

Some mountaineer had tried to establish a claim to the Flat by building a little cabin of sugar pine shakes, and though we had arrived early in the afternoon, I decided to camp here for the night, as the trail was buried in the snow which was about six feet deep, and I wanted to examine the topography and plan our course. Chilwell cleared away the snow from the door and floor of the cabin, and made a bed in it of boughs of fernlike silver fir, though I urged the same sort of bed made under the trees on the snow. But he had the house habit.

After camp arrangements were made, he reminded me of my promise about the gun, hoping eagerly for improvement of our bill of fare, however slight. Accordingly I loaded the gun, paced off thirty yards from the cabin,

or shanty, and told Mr. Chilwell to pin a piece of paper on the wall and see
if I could not put shot into it and prove the gun's worth. So he pinned a
piece of an envelope on the shanty wall and vanished around the corner,
calling out, "Fire away."

I supposed that he had gone some distance back of the cabin, but
instead he went inside of it and stood up against the mark that he had
himself placed on the wall, and as the shake wall of soft sugar pine was only
about half an inch thick, the shot passed through it and into his shoulder.
He came rushing out with his hand on his shoulder, crying in great con-
cern, "You've shot *me*, you've shot *me*, Scottie." The weather being cold, he
fortunately had on three coats and as many shirts. One of the coats was a
heavy English overcoat. I discovered that the shot had passed through all this
clothing and into his shoulder, and the embedded pellets had to be picked
out with the point of a penknife. I asked him how he could be so foolish
as to stand opposite the mark. "Because," he replied, "I never imagined the
blank gun would shoot through the side of the 'ouse."

We found our way easily enough over the deep snow, guided by the
topography, and discovered the trail on the brow of the valley, just as the
Bridal Veil came in sight. I didn't know that it was one of the famous falls I
had read about, and calling Chilwell's attention to it I said, "See that dainty
little fall over there. I should like to camp at the foot of it to see the ferns
and lilies that may be there. It looks small from here, only about fifteen or
twenty feet, but it may be sixty or seventy." So little did we then know of
Yosemite's magnitudes!

After spending eight or ten days in visiting the falls and the high points
of view around the walls, making sketches, collecting flowers and ferns, etc.,
we decided to make the return trip by way of Wawona [Clark's Station],

then owned by Galen Clark, the Yosemite pioneer. The night before the start was made on the return trip, we camped near the Bridal Veil Meadows, where, as we lay eating our suppers by the light of the campfire, we were visited by a brown bear. We heard him approaching by the heavy crackling of twigs. Chilwell, in alarm, after listening a while, said, "I see it! I see it! It's a bear, a grizzly! Where is the gun? You take the gun and shoot him—you can shoot best." But the gun had only a charge of birdshot in it; therefore, while the bear stood on the opposite side of the fire, at a distance of probably twenty-five or thirty feet, I hastily loaded in a lot of buckshot. The buckshot was too large to chamber, and therefore it made a zigzag charge on top of the birdshot charge, the two charges occupying about half of the barrel. Thus armed, the gun held at rest pointed at the bear, we sat hushed and motionless, according to instructions from the man who sold the gun, solemnly waiting and watching, as full of fear as the musket of shot. Finally, after sniffing and whining for his supper what seemed to us a long time, the young, inexperienced bear walked off. We were much afraid of his return to attack us. We did not then know that bears never attack sleeping campers, and dreading another visit, we kept awake on guard most of the night.

Like the Coulterville trail, all the high-lying part of the Mariposa trail was deeply snow-buried, but we found our way without the slightest trouble, steering by the topography in a general way along the brow of the canyon of the south fork of the Merced River, and in a day or two reached Wawona. Here we replenished our little flour sack, and Mr. Clark gave us a piece of bear meat.

We then pushed eagerly on up the Wawona ridge through a magnificent sugar pine forest and into the far-famed Mariposa Sequoia Grove. The sun was down when we entered the Grove, but we soon had a good fire, and at supper that night we tasted bear meat for the first time. My flesh-hungry companion ate it eagerly, though to me it seemed so rank and oily that I was unable to swallow a single morsel.

After supper we replenished the fire and gazed enchanted at the vividly illumined brown boles of the giants towering about us, while the stars sparkled in wonderful beauty above their huge domed heads. We camped here long uncounted days, wandering about from tree to tree, taking no note of time. The longer we gazed the more we admired not only their colossal size, but their majestic beauty and dignity. Greatest of trees, greatest of living things, their noble domes poised in unchanging repose seemed to belong to the sky.

While we camped in the Mariposa Grove, the abundance of bear tracks caused Mr. Chilwell no little alarm, and he proposed that we load the gun properly with buckshot and without any useless birdshot; but there was no means of drawing the charge—it had to be shot off. The recoil was so great that it bruised his shoulder and sent him spinning like a top. Casting down the miserable, kicking, bad-luck musket among the Sequoia cones and branches that littered the ground, he stripped and examined his unfortunate shoulder and, in painful indignation and wrath, found it black and blue and more seriously hurt by the bruising recoil blow than it was by the shot at Crane Flat.

Excerpt of Muir's journal from William Frederic Badè, *The Life and Letters of John Muir*, vol. 1 (Boston: Houghton Mifflin, 1924), 183–88.

SEQUOIA INK

I N THE AUTUMN OF 1870, John Muir headed out of Yosemite Valley, traveling by way of the boulder-choked gorge of the Merced Canyon, detouring through the Merced Grove of sequoia. His decision to leave Yosemite resulted, at least in part, from the amorous advances of Mrs. Thérèse Yelverton, Viscountess Avonmore, which made him uncomfortable. Yelverton supported herself as a travel writer, and she was in Yosemite writing a novel, *Zanita: A Tale of the Yosemite*. Appropriating the inhabitants of Yosemite as characters in the novel, it was Muir who figured prominently as the heroic Kenmuir. From the Merced Grove, Muir wrote the following letter to Jeanne Carr, using ink he crafted from the dark purple resin of a sequoia cone mixed with water, before he headed to Pat Delaney's ranch in La Grange, California, where he remained until spring. This Nut-Time letter was Muir's first acknowledgment of his allegiance to wildness and to the mountains that would not be forgotten as he plowed Delaney's fields.

* * *

SQUIRRELVILLE, SEQUOIA CO., NUT-TIME, [AUTUMN, 1870]

Dear Mrs. Carr:

Do behold the King in his glory, King Sequoia! Behold! Behold! seems all I can say. Some time ago I left all for Sequoia and have been and am at his feet, fasting and praying for light, for is he not the greatest light in the woods, in the world? Where are such columns of sunshine, tangible, accessible, terrestrialized? Well may I fast, not from bread, but from business, book-making, duty-going, and other trifles, and great is my reward already for the manly, treely sacrifice. What giant truths since coming to Gigantea, what magnificent clusters of Sequoic *becauses*. From here I cannot recite you one, for you are down a thousand fathoms deep in dark political quagg, not a burr-length less. But I'm in the woods, woods, woods, and they are in *me-ee-ee*. The King tree and I have sworn eternal love—sworn it without swearing, and I've taken the sacrament with Douglas squirrel, drank Sequoia wine, Sequoia blood, and with its rosy purple drops I am writing this woody gospel-letter.

I never before knew the virtue of Sequoia juice. Seen with sunbeams in it, its color is the most royal of all royal purples. No wonder the Indians instinctively drink it, for they know not what. I wish I was so drunk with Sequoical that I could preach the green-brown woods to all the juiceless world, descending from this divine wilderness like a John [the] Baptist, eating Douglas squirrels and wild honey or wild anything, crying, "Repent, for the Kingdom of Sequoia is at hand!"

There is balm in these leafy Gileads—pungent burrs and living

King-juice for all defrauded civilization; for sick grangers and politicians; no need of Salt rivers. Sick or successful, come suck Sequoia and be saved.

Douglas squirrel is so pervaded with rosin and burr juice his flesh can scarce be eaten even by mountaineers—no wonder he is so charged with magnetism! One of the little lions ran across my feet the other day as I lay resting under a fir, and the effect was a thrill like a battery shock. I would eat him no matter how rosiny for the lightning he holds. I wish I could eat wilder things. Think of the grouse with balsam-scented crop stored with spruce buds, the wild sheep full of glacier meadow grass and daisies azure, and the bear burly and brown as Sequoia, eating pine-burrs and wasps stings and all; then think of the soft lightningless poultice-like pap reeking upon town tables. No wonder cheeks and legs become flabby and fungoid! I wish I were wilder, and so, bless Sequoia, I will be. There is at least a punky spark in my heart, and it may blaze in this autumn gold, fanned by the King. Some of my grandfathers must have been born on a Muirland for there is heather in me and tinctures of bog juices that send me to *Cassiope*, and oozing through all my veins, impel me unhaltingly through endless glacier meadows, seemingly the deeper and danker the better.

See Sequoia aspiring in the upper skies, every summit modeled in fine cycloidal curves, as if pressed into unseen moulds, every bole warm in the mellow amber sun. How truly godful in mien! I was talking the other day with a duchess and was struck with the grand bow with which she bade me goodbye and thanked me for the glaciers I gave her, but this forenoon King Sequoia bowed to me down in the grove as I stood gazing, and the highbred gestures of the lady seemed rude by contrast.[1]

There goes Squirrel Douglas, the master-spirit of the tree-top. It has just occurred to me how his belly is buffy brown and his back silver gray.

Ever since the first Adam of his race saw trees and burrs, his belly has been rubbing upon buff bark, and his back has been combed with silver needles. Would that some of you wise—terribly wise—social scientists might discover some method of living as true to nature as the buff people of the woods, running as free as the winds and waters among the burrs and filbert thickets of these leafy, mothery woods.

The sun is set, and the star candles are being lighted to show me and Douglas squirrel to bed. Therefore, my Carr, goodnight. You say, "When are you coming down?" Ask the Lord—Lord Sequoia.

John Muir

"John Muir to Jeanne C. Carr, Squirrelville, Sequoia Co., Nut-Time, Autumn 1870," John Muir Papers, Holt-Atherton Department of Special Collections, University of the Pacific Library © 1984 Muir-Hanna Trust.

EMERSON, KEEP YOUR NOSE
OUT OF DOORS

IN SPEAKING BEFORE THE American Alpine Club in 1911,
John Muir reminisced about his youth, his mountaineering prowess, and Ralph Waldo Emerson. Emerson had visited
Yosemite in May 1871. Too shy to approach him, Muir sent
a note to Emerson entreating him to extend his stay in the
Valley. Climbing up the hen-ladder into the hang nest Muir
had built onto the side of Hutchings's sawmill, Emerson was
impressed with Muir's collection of plant specimens, sketches,
and journals. Proposing a camping trip into the heart of the
mountains, the most Muir could expect was to accompany
Emerson and his party on their way out of the Valley on the
condition that Emerson camp one night with him in the
Mariposa Grove. Emerson's enthusiasm for camping out was
dampened when fear for his health and safety precluded the
plan. He stayed at Clark's Station, though Muir was certain
that fresh air and pine boughs were better for Emerson than
carpet dust.

In later years Muir recalled the two most significant

moments in his life were the discovery of the *Calypso borealis* in the Canada swamp and his meeting with Emerson. Muir's mention of Emerson in his speech recalled his regret that they were not able to camp together.[1]

* * *

I went into the Yosemite forty-three years ago last April [1868]. I had just arrived in California from Florida and Cuba by the way of New York and Panama, and went directly to the Yosemite Valley.

When I had been there two years, [Ralph Waldo] Emerson came in with his son and Prof. Thayer. I saw a good deal of Emerson; he came to see me every day.

I made a thousand dollars by working in a sawmill while I was in the Yosemite during these years.

In the whole Sierra there isn't a sneeze, but I was quite unable to convince Emerson that this was so. Although I tried my best, I could not persuade him to sleep out of doors the night that we visited the Wawona grove of big trees. He and those with him had formed the house habit beyond all possibility of change. He feared some mysterious influence of the night air. My father had the same idea. To think of that being a Scotch habit! I long had the idea of writing a book to be called: "Keep your nose out of doors." I was seventeen hours on Mount Shasta once, in a snow storm, in my shirt sleeves, and took no harm from it. There was something very queer about that storm; it was accompanied by awful thunder ("the most tremendously loud and appalling ever heard").

To me timber-line and bread-line were synonymous. On my tramps in the Sierra, I carried a bag of bread; this when descending I always rolled downhill ahead of me, so it soon became a bag of bread crumbs. This lasted me three weeks. I first dried it out thoroughly, and it would then, with care, keep for any length of time without getting mouldy.

To my father who was solicitous lest the devil should misguide my steps, I once wrote, "Father, don't trouble yourself about the devil so far as I am concerned. The devil never gets above timber-line."

In my camps at timber-line, I would keep a fire going all night, made from the pitchy roots of the *Albicaulis* pine. I would seek shelter under the lee of these dwarf pines, which grow so solidly matted and packed together, like the top of a spruce or hemlock hedge, that one could walk on their tops without sinking through. The wind always draws downhill at night on the mountains, so one could seek shelter with entire assurance as to which way it was going to blow. Having no blanket I could sleep only twenty minutes to a half hour at a time before I would be awakened by the cold. I would start up the fire and get a little warmed, and then try it again, and so wear the night out. When I was asleep, one side of me roasted, while the other froze. In the morning I was naturally stiff and cold, but soon from the effect of tea and sunshine I felt "lifted up." It was physiological radium, Scotch radium. My impulse then was to run and shout.

You can't take cold if you keep your nose out of doors. In Alaska, once I spent nine days on the ice. It was all a delight to me. It was a wonder how a creature with so slight sustenance could be so glad. I caught cold once after such a trip. To cure it, I plunged into a pool of ice water and then into a bearskin bag. It was a complete cure. No microbe could stand that.

Excerpt from John Muir, "A Talk by John Muir After a Dinner Given to Him and Certain Members of the American Alpine Club by Judge Harrington Putnam at the Manhattan Hotel, New York, June 17, 1911, from Notes by Alden Sampson," *Sierra Club Bulletin* 12 (January 1924): 43–46.

TUOLUMNE CANYON

LEAVING LA GRANGE, CALIFORNIA, in May 1869, John Muir traveled east, accompanying shepherd Billy Simms and Pat Delaney's sheep to pasture in Tuolumne Meadows above Yosemite Valley. Muir would oversee Billy, while Billy looked after the sheep, giving Muir time to explore and study plants, though he knew nothing of the place they were going. They headed east into the Yosemite Creek Basin above Yosemite's north wall. Two miles from the brink of Yosemite Valley, the sheep grazed. Moving on to Tuolumne Meadows, there they remained throughout the summer. In August 1869, Muir explored the Tuolumne River to the west below Soda Springs and obtained his first partial view of the Tuolumne Canyon.

In early November 1871, Muir made a final trip of the season. He headed north out of Yosemite Valley, trekked up beyond the Yosemite Creek Basin, and reached the brow of the Tuolumne Canyon that he had observed in 1869. The gorge dropped down more than four thousand feet into the canyon. Bounding over the rim of the wall, Muir reached the

Tuolumne River and followed the river down to the Hetch Hetchy Valley. Through the edge of a storm, he returned to Yosemite Valley.

* * *

Like the Merced, the Tuolumne River also falls rapidly at first, making a descent of about three thousand feet in the first three miles of its course. It then enters one of the very noblest canyon-valleys of the range. It extends northward for a distance of about eight miles, then suddenly bends westward and widens into a broad, flat-bottomed valley, created by the force of the confluent ice-streams that once descended from the flanks of Mounts Dana, Gibbs, and other nameless mountains to the south of Gibbs, and formed a vast *mer de glace*, four or five miles in width. This ice-sea had two principal outlets: one on the south side of the Hoffman range, by which an immense flood of ice passed over the present water-divide into the Merced basin, and into the Yosemite Valley, which it entered by the Tenaya Canyon; the other, on the north side of the Hoffman range, through the Great Tuolumne Canyon, which begins here, and extends westward unbrokenly a distance of more than twenty miles, varying in depth from two thousand to five thousand feet. From the foot of the Great Canyon down to the San Joaquin plain and across it to the San Joaquin River, the Tuolumne flows through valleys and canyons in every way similar to those of the Merced below Yosemite.

Sometime in August, in the year 1869, in following the river three or four miles below the Soda Springs, I obtained a partial view of the Great Tuolumne Canyon before I had heard of its existence. The following winter I read what the State Geologist wrote concerning it:

> *"The river enters a canyon which is about twenty miles long, and*
> *probably inaccessible through its entire length. . . . It certainly cannot be*
> *entered from its head. Mr. [Clarence] King followed this canyon down*
> *as far as he could, to where the river precipitated itself down in a grand*
> *fall over a mass of rock so rounded on the edge that it was impossi-*
> *ble for him to approach near enough to look over. Where the canyon*
> *opens out again twenty miles below, so as to be accessible, a remarkable*
> *counterpart to Yosemite is found, called the Hetch-Hetchy Valley. . . .*
> *Between this and Soda Springs there is a descent in the river of for-*
> *ty-five hundred feet, and what grand waterfalls and stupendous scenery*
> *there may be here, it is not easy to say. . . . Adventurous climbers . . .*
> *should try to penetrate into this unknown gorge, which perhaps may*
> *admit of being entered through some of the side canyons coming in*
> *from the north."*

Since that time, I have entered the Great Canyon from the north by three different side-canyons, and have passed through it from end to end, entering at the Hetch-Hetchy Valley and coming out at the Big Meadows below the Soda Springs, without encountering any extraordinary difficulties. I am sure that it may be entered at more than fifty different points along the walls by mountaineers of ordinary nerve and skill. At the head, it is easily accessible on both sides.

In September, 1871, I began a careful exploration of all the mountain basins whose waters pass through the Yosemite Valley, where I had remained winter and summer for two years. I did not go to them for a Saturday, or a Sunday, or a stingy week, but with unmeasured time and independent of companions or scientific associations. As I climbed out of Yosemite to begin my glorious toil, I gloated over the numberless streams I would have to follow to their hidden sources in wild, untrodden canyons, over the unnumbered and nameless mountains I would have to climb and account for—over the glacial rivers whose history I would have to trace, in hieroglyphics of sculptured rocks, forests, lakes, and meadows.

This was my "method of study": I drifted about from rock to rock, from stream to stream, from grove to grove. Where night found me, there I camped. When I discovered a new plant, I sat down beside it for a minute or a day, to make its acquaintance and hear what it had to tell. When I came to moraines or ice-scratches upon the rocks, I traced them back, learning what I could of the glacier that made them. I asked the boulders I met, whence they came and whither they were going. I followed to their fountains the traces of the various soils upon which forests and meadows are planted; and when I discovered a mountain or rock of marked form and structure, I climbed about it, comparing it with its neighbors, marking its relations to living or dead glaciers, streams of water, avalanches of snow, etc., in seeking to account for its existence and character. It is astonishing how high and far we can climb in mountains that we love. Weary at times, with only the birds and squirrels to compare notes with, I rested beneath the spicy pines, among the needles and burs, or upon the plushy sod of a glacier meadow, touching my cheek to its enameling gentians and daisies, in order to absorb their magnetism or mountainism. No evil consequence from "waste of time," concerning which good people who accomplish nothing make such a sermonizing has, thus far, befallen me.

Early one afternoon, when my mountain freedom was about a week old, after drifting among the picturesque domes and ridges of the west rim of Yosemite Creek basin, I struck its northernmost tributary—a lovely stream in rapids and bonny cascades, and from the abundance of moraine soil through which it flows, everywhere green and flowery. As I followed it up to its head, wading across spongy patches of meadow and climbing over fallen logs and heaps of boulders, to the top of the Yosemite Creek divide, I felt the premonition of discovery. I found that here it was not a thin ridge, but a smooth, sedgy tableland, holding a shallow mirror-lake. A few yards from the margin, on a gravelly hillock, covered with a beautiful grove of the Williamson spruce (*Abies hookeriana*), I made my camp, and then proceeded to explore the plateau in a north-easterly direction. I had not gone far before I came in sight of a stately group of headlands, arching gracefully on the south, with here and there a feathery pine tree on their sides, but vertical and bare on the north. They are drawn up side-by-side in exact order, their necks stiffly curved, like high-mettled cavalry horses ready for a charge. From the base of their precipitous fronts there extends a large, shallow mountain-bowl, in the bottom of which ten smaller bowls have been scooped, each forming the basin of a bright lakelet, abundantly fringed with spruce trees and bordered close to the water with yellow sedge. Looking northward from the edge of the great lake-bowl, I observed several gaps that seemed to sink suddenly, suggesting the existence of a deep gorge running at right-angles to their courses, and I began to guess that I was near the rim of the Great Tuolumne Canyon. I looked back at the wild headlands and down at the ten lakes and northward among the gaps, veering for some minutes like a confused compass needle. When I settled to a steady course, it was to follow a ridge-top that extends from near the edge of the lake-bowl in a direction a little east of north, and to find it terminating suddenly in a sheer front over four thousand feet in depth.

This stupendous precipice forms a portion of the south wall of the Great Tuolumne Canyon, about halfway between the head and foot. Until I had reached this brink, I could obtain only narrow strips and wedges of landscape through gaps in the trees; but now the view was bounded only by the sky. Never have I beheld a nobler atlas of mountains. A thousand pictures composed that one mountain countenance, glowing with the Holy Spirit of Light! I crept along on the rugged edge of the wall until I found a place where I could sit down to absorb the glorious landscape in safety. The Tuolumne River shimmered and spangled below, showing two or three miles of its length, curving past sheer precipices and meandering through groves and small oval meadows. Its voice I distinctly heard, giving no tidings of heavy falls; but cascade tones, and those of foaming rapids, were in it, fused into harmony as smooth as the wind-music of the pines.

The opposite wall of the canyon, mainly made up of the ends of ridges shorn off abruptly by the great Tuolumne glacier that once flowed past them, presents a series of elaborately sculptured precipices, like those of Yosemite Valley. Yet, sublime as is the scenery of this magnificent canyon, it offers no violent contrasts to the rest of the landscape; for the mountains beyond rise gradually higher in corresponding grandeur, and tributary canyons come in from the ice-fountains of the summits that are every way worthy of the trunk canyon. Many a spiry peak rises in sharp relief against the sky; in front are domes innumerable and broad, whale-backed ridges, darkly fringed about their bases with pines, through openings in which I could here and there discern the green of meadows and the flashes of bright eye-lakes. There was no stretching away of any part of this divine landscape into dimness, nor possible division of it into back, and middle, and foreground. All its mountains appeared equally near, like the features of one face, on which the sun was gazing kindly, ripening and mellowing it like autumn fruit.

The forces that shaped the mountains—grinding out canyons and lake-basins, sharpening peaks and crests, digging out domes from the inclosing rocks—carving their plain flanks into their present glorious forms, may be seen at their work at many points in the high Sierra. From where I was seated, sphinx-like, on the brink of the mighty wall, I had extensive views of the channels of five immense tributary glaciers that came in from the summits toward the north-east. Everyone of these five ice-rivers had been sufficiently powerful to thrust their heads down into the very bottom of the main Tuolumne glacier. I could also trace portions of the courses of smaller tributaries, whose canyons terminated a thousand feet above the bottom of the trunk canyon. So fully are the lives of these vanished glaciers recorded upon the clean, unblurred pages of the mountains, that it is difficult to assure ourselves that we do not actually see them and feel their icy breath. As I gazed, notwithstanding the kindly sunshine, the waving of grass, and the humming of flies, the stupendous canyon at my feet filled again with creeping ice, winding in sublime curves around massive mountain brows; its white surface sprinkled with many a gray boulder and traversed with many a yawning *crevasse*. The wide basins of the summits were heaped with fountain-snow, glowing white in the thin sunshine, or blue in the shadows cast from black, spiry peaks.

The last days of this glacial winter are not yet past, so young is our world. I used to envy the father of our race, dwelling as he did in contact with the new-made fields and plants of Eden; but I do so no more because I have discovered that I also live in "creation's dawn." The morning stars still sing together, and the world, not yet half made, becomes more beautiful every day.

By the time the glaciers were melted from my mind, the sun was nearing the horizon. Looking once more at the Tuolumne, glistening far beneath, I was seized with an invincible determination to descend the canyon wall to the bottom. Unable to discover any way that I cared to try, from where I stood, I ran back along the ridge by which I approached the valley, then westward about a mile, and clambered out upon another point that stood boldly forward into the canyon. From here I had a commanding view of a small side-canyon on my left, running down at a steep angle; which I judged, from the character of the opposite wall, might possibly be practicable all the way. Then I hastened back among the latest sun-shadows to my camp in the spruce trees, resolved to make an attempt to penetrate the heart of the Great Canyon next day. I awoke early, breakfasted, and waited for the dawn. The thin air was frosty, but knowing that I would be warm in climbing, I tightened my belt and set out in my shirt-sleeves, limb-loose as a pugilist. By the time I reached the mouth of the narrow canyon-way I had chosen, the sun had touched all the peaks with beamless light. I was exhilarated by the pure, divine wildness that imbued mountain and sky, and I could not help shouting as I dashed down the topmost curves of the canyon, there covered with a dense plush of *carex*, easy and pleasant to the tread.

After accomplishing a descent of four or five hundred feet, I came to a small mirror-lake set here on the slanting face of the canyon upon a kind of shelf. This side-canyon was formed by a small glacier, tributary to the main Tuolumne glacier, which, in its descent, met here with a very hard seamless bar of granite that extended across its course, compelling it to rise, while the softer granite in front of it was eroded and carried away, thus forming a basin for the waters of the canyon stream. The bar or dam is beautifully molded and polished, giving evidence of tremendous pressure. Below the lake, both the sides and bottom of the canyon became rougher, and I was compelled to scramble down and around a large number of small precipices, fifty or a hundred feet high, that crossed the canyon, one above another, like gigantic stairs.

Below the foot of the stairs are extensive willow-tangles, growing upon rough slopes of sharp-angled rocks, through which the stream mumbles and gropes its way, most of the time out of sight. These tangles are too dense to walk *among*, even if they grew upon a smooth bottom, and too tall and flexible to walk *upon*. Crinkled and loosely felted as they are by the pressure of deep snow for half the year, they form more impenetrable jungles than I ever encountered in the swamps of Florida. In descending, one may possibly tumble and crush over them in some way, but to ascend them, with their longer branches presented against you like bayonets, is very nearly impossible. In the midst of these tangles and along their margins, small garden-like meadows occur where the stream has been able to make a level deposit of soil. . . . In these moist garden-patches, so thoroughly hidden, the bears like to wallow like hogs. I found many places that morning where the bent and squeezed sedges showed that I had disturbed them and knew I was likely at any moment to come upon a cross mother with her cubs. Below the region of bear-gardens and willow-tangles, the canyon becomes narrow and smooth, the smoothness being due to the action of snow-avalanches that sweep down from the mountains above and pour through this steep and narrow portion like torrents of water.

I had now accomplished a descent of nearly twenty-five hundred feet from the top, and there remained about two thousand feet to be accomplished before I reached the river. As I descended this smooth portion, I

found that its bottom became more and more steeply inclined, and I halted
to scan it closely, hoping to discover some way of avoiding it altogether
by passing around on either of the sides. But this I quickly decided to be
impossible, the sides being apparently as bare and seamless as the bottom.
I then began to creep down the smooth incline, depending mostly upon
my hands, wetting them with my tongue, and striking them flatly upon the
rock to make them stick by atmospheric pressure. In this way I very nearly
reached a point where a seam comes down to the bottom in an easy slope,
which would enable me to escape to a portion of the main wall that I knew
must be climbable from the number of live oak bushes growing upon it.
But after cautiously measuring the steepness—scrutinizing it again and
again, and trying my wet hands upon it—both mind and limbs declared
it unsafe, for the least slip would insure a tumble of hundreds of feet. I
was, therefore, compelled to retrace my devious slides and leaps up the
canyon, making a vertical rise of about five hundred feet, in order that I
might reach a point where I could climb out to the main canyon wall;
my only hope of reaching the bottom that day being by picking my way
down its face. I knew from my observations of the previous day that this
portion of the canyon was crossed by well-developed planes of cleavage
that prevented the formation of smooth, vertical precipices of more than
a few hundred feet in height and the same in width. These may usually
be passed without much difficulty. After two or three hours more of hard
scrambling, I at length stood among cool shadows on the riverbank, in
the heart of the great unexplored canyon, having made a descent of about
forty-five hundred feet, the bottom of this portion of the canyon above the
level of the sea being quite forty-six hundred feet. The canyon is here fully
two hundred yards wide (about twice the size of the Merced at Yosemite),

and timbered richly with libocedrus and pine. A beautiful reach stretches away from where I sat resting, its border-trees leaning toward each other, making a long arched lane, down which the joyous waters sung in foaming rapids. Stepping out of the river-grove to a small sandy flat, I obtained a general view of the canyon walls, rising to a height of from four thousand to five thousand feet, composed of rocks of every form of which Yosemites are made. About a mile up the canyon, on the south side, there is a most imposing rock, nearly related in form to the Yosemite Half Dome. The side-canyon by which I descended looked like an insignificant notch or groove in the main wall, though not less than seven hundred or eight hundred feet deep in most places.

Immediately opposite the point I descended are "royal arches," like those of Yosemite, formed by the breaking-up and removal of a portion of a number of the concentric layers of a dome. All of the so-called "royal arches" of this region are produced in the same way.

About a mile farther down the canyon, I came to the mouth of a tributary that enters the trunk canyon on the north. Its glacier must have been of immense size, for it eroded its channel down to a level with the bottom of the main canyon.

I pushed on down the canyon a couple of miles farther, passing over leafy level floors, buried in shady greenwood, and over hot sandy flats. . . . Tall grasses brushed my shoulders, and yet taller lilies and columbines rung their bells above my head. Nor was there any lack of familiar birds and flies, bees and butterflies. Myriads of sunny wings stirred all the air into music. The stellar-jay, garrulous and important, flitted from pine to pine; squirrels were gathering nuts; woodpeckers hammered the dead limbs; water-ouzels sung divinely on wet boulders among the rapids; and the robin-redbreast of the orchards was everywhere. . . . Among these mighty cliffs and domes there is no word of chaos or of desolation; every rock is as elaborately and thoughtfully carved and finished as a crystal or shell.

I followed the river three miles. In this distance it makes a vertical descent of about three hundred feet, which it accomplishes by rapids. I would fain have lingered here for months, could I have lived with the bears on cherries and berries, and found bedding and blanketing like theirs. I thought of trying their board and lodging for a few days; but at length, as I was in my shirt-sleeves and without food, I began my retreat. Let those who become breathless in ascending a few stairs think of climbing these Yosemite attics to a bed five thousand feet above the basement. I pushed up the first three thousand feet almost without stopping to take breath, making only momentary halts to look at striated surfaces, or to watch the varying appearances of peaks and domes as they presented themselves at different points.

As I neared the summit I became very tired, and the last thousand feet seemed long indeed, although I began to rest frequently, turning to see the setting sun feeding the happy rosy mountains. I reached the top of the wall at sunset; then I had only to skim heedlessly along a smooth horizontal mile to camp. I made a fire and cooked my supper, which, with me, means steeping a tin-cupful of tea and eating a craggy boulder of bread. How few experience profound mountain weariness and mountain hunger!

The life of a mountaineer is favorable to the development of soul-life, as well as limb-life, each receiving abundance of exercise and abundance of food. We little suspect the great capacity that our flesh has for knowledge. Oftentimes in climbing canyon walls I have come to polished slopes near the heads of precipices that seemed to be too steep to be ventured upon.

After scrutinizing them and carefully noting every dint and scratch that might give hope for a foothold, I have decided that they were unsafe. Yet my limbs, possessing a separate sense, would be of a different opinion, after they also had examined the descent and confidently have set out to cross the condemned slopes against the remonstrances of my other will. My legs sometimes transport me to camp, in the darkness, over cliffs, and through bogs and forests that are inaccessible to city legs during the day, even when piloted by the mind which owns them. In like manner the soul sets forth at times upon rambles of its own. Brooding over some vast mountain landscape, or among the spiritual countenances of mountain flowers, our bodies disappear, our mortal coils come off without any shuffling, and we blend into the rest of Nature, utterly blind to the boundaries that measure human quantities into separate individuals. But it is after both the body and soul of a mountaineer have worked hard, and enjoyed much, that they are most palpably separate. Our weary limbs, lying restingly among the pine needles, make no attempt to follow after or sympathize with the nimble spirit that, apparently glad of the opportunity, runs off alone down the steep gorges, along the beetling cliffs, or away among the peaks and glaciers of the farthest landscapes, or into realms that eye hath not seen, nor ear heard; and when at length we are ready to return home to our other self, we scarcely for a moment know in what direction to seek for it. I have often been unable to make my muscles move at such times. I have ordered my body to rise and go to bed, when it seemed to me as if the nerves concerned were cut, and that my soul-telegram had not reached the muscles at all.

The next morning after my raid in the Tuolumne country, I passed back over the border to Merced, glad that I had seen so much, and glad that so much was so little of the whole. The grand rocks, I said, of this Tuolumne Yosemite are books never yet opened; and after studying the mountains of the Merced basin, I shall go to them as to a library, where all kinds of rock structure and rock formation will be explained, and where I shall yet discover a thousand waterfalls.

Excerpt from John Muir, "Explorations in the Great Tuolumne Cañon," *Overland Monthly* 11 (August 1873): 139–47.

CHRISTMAS SHEEP

AFTER JOHN MUIR'S FINAL EXCURSION of the season into the Tuolumne Canyon, he returned to Yosemite Valley and spent the winter of 1871 in a cabin at Black's Hotel. He worked as a caretaker for the hotel proprietors, A. G. Black and his wife, who had become friends with Muir. Muir wrote to Jeanne Carr that he had resigned his position as a sawyer for James M. Hutchings, and he intended to have no further dealings with him. In writing to his mother, Ann G. Muir, he noted that travel had ceased for the season and that he had been "sleeping in the rocks and snow, often weary and hungry, sustained by the excitement of my subject. . . . For the last few days I have been eating and resting and enjoying long warm sleeps beneath a roof, in a warm, rockless, boulderless bed." At Black's Hotel, under the shadow of Sentinel Rock, Muir had ample time to compile the notes he had written while studying the glacial structure over which he had trodden. He began to write for publication. Muir's first article on the glacial formation of Yosemite Valley appeared in the *New York Tribune*. As a result of its success, he thought he might earn a living as a writer. The second article recounted daily activities in Yosemite and put a humorous spin on a glimpse into life in the Valley.[1]

* * *

Yo-Semite Valley, Jan. 1, [1872].

Winter has taken Yo-Semite, and we are snowbound. The latest leaves are shaken from the oaks and alders; the snow-laden pines, with drooping boughs, look like barbed-arrows aimed at the sky, and the fern-tangles and meadows are spread with a smooth cloth of snow. Our latest visitor fled two weeks ago. He came via Mariposa and was safely conducted over the mountain snows by Galen Clark, the well-known pioneer and guardian of the Valley. The total number of visitors to the valley in 1870 was nearly 1,700, which was about 600 more than on any previous year. This season, about 2,150 entered the valley.

All of our landlords, except one, have disappeared, and doubtless are engaged in concert with stage and railroad companies, with next year's problems of travel, sorting their labyrinth of tolls and trails. . . . The 20th of November first brought us signs of winter. Broad, fibrous arcs of white clouds spanned the valley from wall to wall; grand island-like masses, bred among the upper domes and brows, wavered doubtfully up and down, some of them suddenly devoured by a swoop of thirsty wind; others, waxing to grand proportions, drifted loosely and heavily about like bergs in a calm sea, or jammed and wedged themselves among spiry crests, or, drawing themselves out like woolen rolls, muffled the highest brows, sometimes leaving bare summits cut off from the walls with pine trees atop, that seemed to float loose as the clouds. Tissiack [Half Dome] was compassed by a soft, furry cloud, upon which her dome seemed to repose clear and warm in yellow light. At the end of these transition days, the whole company of valley clouds were marshaled for storm; they fused close and blended, until every seam and bay of blue sky was shut, and our temple, throughout all of its cells and halls, was smoothly full. Rain and snow fell steadily for three days, beginning Nov. 24, giving about four feet of snow to the valley rim. The snow line descended to the bottom of the valley on the night of Nov. 25, but after-rains prevented any considerable accumulation.

Then the rocks began to fall. During our equable rainless summers, atmospheric disintegration goes on with the greatest gentleness, and scarce a rock is cast down, but the first rains find many a huge mass ripe for change, and after-slopes are made slippery, seams washed out, and water-wedges driven. Constant thunder proclaims the magnitude of accomplished work. We ran repeatedly from the house to hear the larger masses journeying down with a tread that shook the valley.

This three days' chapter of rain was underscored by a seam of sunshine half a day in width, beneath which darkness began to gather for a chapter of snow; heavy cloud-masses rolled down the black-washed walls, circling cathedral rocks and domes, and hiding off all the upper brows and peaks. Thin strips of sunshine slid through momentary seams that were quickly blinded out. The darkness deepened for hours, until every separating shade and line were dimmed to equal black, and all the bright air of our gulf was sponged up and fastened windless and pulseless in universal cloud. "It's bound to snow," said a mountaineer to me, as he gazed into the heavy gloom, "bound to snow, when it gathers cloud material gradual as this. We'll have a reg'lar old-fashioned storm afore long." Scarce had he delivered himself of this meteorological prophecy, ere the beginning flakes appeared, journeying tranquilly down with waving, slow-circling gestures, easy and confident, as if long familiar with the paths of sky. Before dark they accomplished a most glorious work of gentle, noiseless beauty. Twelve inches of snow fell during the night, and when morning opened our temple, there was more of beauty than pen can tell—from meadow to summit, from wall to wall, every tree, and bush, and sculptured rock was muffled and dazzled in downy, unbroken, undrifted snow. Transparent film-clouds hung in the open azure, or draped the walls, the gray granite showing dimly through their fairy veil. This after-storm gauze is formed when vapor is made by sun-rays upon exposed portions of the wet walls, which is of higher temperature than the air with which it drifts into contact.

One day usually is sufficient to dry the warmest portions of the walls, and to lave and mix the air, until it is about equal in temperature to the rocks which contain it—then that rocky storm-tissue disappears. After every heavy snow-fall, numerous avalanches are born upon all of the slopes and canyons of suitable steepness. In general appearance, they resemble waterfalls of the highest free-falling kind, being like them, close, opaque, white in color, and composed of companies of comets shooting downward with unequal velocity, amid a casing atmosphere of whirling dust. They are most numerous about the slopes of Glacier Point and Tissiack, but by far the grandest avalanches of this Yo-Semite region are those of Cloud's Rest, on the north side, up Tenaya Canyon.

Yo-Semite and we slid smoothly over the astronomical edge of '71; Santa Claus came with very little ado, gave trinkets to our half-dozen younglings, and dropped crusted cakes into bachelors' cabins; but upon the whole, our holidays were sorry, unhilarious, whiskyfied affairs. A grand intercampal

Christmas dinner was devised, on a scale and style becoming our peerless valley; heaps of solemn substantials were to be lightened and broidered with cookies and backed by countless cakes, blocky and big as boulders, and a craggy trough-shaped pie was planned for heart and soul of the feast. It was to have formed a rough model of Yo-Semite, with domes and brows of "duff" and falls of guttering gravy. "South dome be mine," cried one, "softened with sauce of Pohono." "I'll eat Royal Arches," cried another, "salted with Bachelors' Tears"; "And I'll choose Riverbank Meadow, plummed with avalanche boulders"; "Pure purple granite for me, cut smooth from the cheek of El Capitan," &c, &c.—all very well conceived; but alack! like all other ladyless feasts, it was a failure. . . . Of course you will guess that in our glorious home we gather on the meadow when our work is done, to feast on the moonlit rocks or dark pines spiring up in the stars, and to drink song from the falls like water, and breathe the deep spirit-hush of the winter. But alas! No! We only quarrel, and gossip. . . . And, to show you how much our rocks and quarrels correspond in magnitude, I will give you our last in detail, which is, perhaps, one of average size.

At the close of this last visiting season, each hotel-keeper found among his remaining provisions a living mutton, and it was desirable that these three sheep should be kept over Winter in the valley to be in readiness for the first pilgrim customers of '72. Now, in Winters of ordinary severity, sheep can care for themselves with but little attention from the shepherd; and at first our sheep seemed to have promise of a mild Winter. They had rich, sunny days with noontimes dreamily warm. They nibbled the willow bushes on the meadows and silver lupines beneath the pines, and gathered bunch grass and late eriogonums up on the rugged debris, but a month ago, when heavy snow fell, they had to be cared for, and trouble began. The three shepherds were equally concerned in the three sheep, and bickerings arose about turns in hunting them up; also about the depth of snow which rendered hunting them up necessary, Black's shepherd holding, with characteristic obstinacy, that in light storms the sheep were better let alone to nibble a living from chaparral in the ice of big rocks. Also, it was proposed that when they were driven up, instead of outraging their gregarious instincts by compelling each to eat his bog sedges in solitude, they should be kept together and "boarded round" from barn to barn. But this union could not be effected because the three sheep were not equal in size, and moreover, Mr. Black's hay was cut on the Bridal Veil Meadow, while Mr. L.'s [Leidig's] was cut on the Bachelor's Tears, and it was argued that one ton of Bachelor's Tears hay was worth two tons of Bridal Veil, because the Bachelor's Tears was sweet, while the Bridal Veil article was boggy and sour. Black's shepherd denied all this, affirming that Bridal Veil carex was good as Bachelor's Tears carex, or Virgin's Tears carex, or any other in the valley, salt or sour. The geographical position of H.'s [James M. Hutchings's] meadow midway between the Veil and Tears, determined the quality of its carex as medium. These bickerings increased in acrimony, and as Black's shepherd was Scotch, L.'s Dutch, and H.'s Yankee, there was grave danger of a war of races, but by brain-racking diplomacy, and a profusion of bloodless blixen, our pastoral sky was cleared, and now all goes heartily well, and each sheep eats its own sedge, in its own barn, tended by its own shepherd.

Excerpt from John Muir, "In the Yo-Semite. Holidays Among the Rocks. Wild Weather—A Picturesque Christmas Dinner—Idyllic Amusements—Poetic Storms—A Paradise of Clouds. Yo-Semite Valley, January 1," *New York Weekly Tribune* (March 13, 1872): 3, cols. 4–5.

LIVING GLACIERS

INFLUENCED BY THE WORK of Louis Agassiz, who published his definitive work on glaciers in 1840 in which he noted that not books but experience was where answers to science resided, John Muir intensified his own empirical study of glaciers in 1872 in Yosemite Valley and the High Sierra. Through his observations of deposits of glacial silt and striations etched into the granite walls and in outlining the routes that carried the glaciers, Muir concluded that glacial action had formed Yosemite Valley. Intent on studying the movement of glacial ice, on August 21 of that year, he spent three days planting stakes on the Maclure Glacier with Galen Clark and Dr. Joseph LeConte, professor of geology at the University of California. Muir returned on October 6 to examine the stakes and planned to continue his studies until it began to snow. Writing to Jeanne Carr on October 8, he described his October excursion. The letter to Carr is followed here by Muir's article that was published several years later on the living glaciers he explored in 1872.

* * *

LETTER TO JEANNE CARR

Yosemite Valley, October 8, 1872

Dear Mrs. Carr:

Here we are again, and here is your letter of Sept. 24th. I got down last evening, and boo! was I not weary after pushing through the rough upper half of the great Tuolumne Canyon? I have climbed more than twenty-four thousand feet in these ten days, three times to the top of the glacieret of Mount Hoffman, and once to Mounts Lyell and Maclure. I have bagged a quantity of Tuolumne rocks sufficient to build a dozen Yosemites; strips of cascades longer than ever, lacy or smooth and white as pressed snow; a glacier basin with ten glassy lakes set all near together like eggs in a nest; then El Capitan and a couple of Tissiacks, canyons glorious with yellows and reds of mountain maple and aspen, and honeysuckle and ash and new indescribable music immeasurable from strange waters and winds, and glaciers, too, flowing and grinding, alive as any on earth. Shall I pull you out some? . . . Here is a cascade two hundred feet wide, half a mile long, glancing this way and that, filled with bounce and dance and joyous hurrah, yet earnest as tempest, and singing like angels loose on a frolic from heaven; and here are more cascades and more, broad and flat like clouds and fringed like flowing hair, with occasional falls erect as pines, and lakes like glowing eyes; and here are visions and dreams, and a splendid set of ghosts, too many for ink and narrow paper.

As for the living "glaciers of the Sierras," here is what I have learned concerning them.

One of the yellow days of last October, when I was among the mountains of the Merced Group, following the footprints of the ancient glaciers that once flowed grandly from their ample fountains, reading what I could of their history as written in moraines and canyons and lakes and carved rocks, I came upon a small stream that was carrying mud I had not before seen. In a calm place where the stream widened I collected some of this mud and observed that it was entirely mineral in composition and fine as flour, like the mud from a fine-grit grindstone. Before I had time to reason I said, *Glacier mud, mountain meal.*

Then I observed that this muddy stream issued from a bank of fresh quarried stones and dirt that was sixty or seventy feet in height. This I at once took to be a moraine. In climbing to the top of it I was struck with the steepness of its slope and with its raw, unsettled, plantless, newborn appearance.

When I had scrambled to the top of the moraine, I saw what seemed a huge snowbank four or five hundred yards in length by half a mile in width. Imbedded in its stained and furrowed surface were stones and dirt like that of which the moraine was built. Dirt-stained lines curved across the snowbank from side to side, and when I observed that these curved lines coincided with the curved moraine and that the stones and dirt were most abundant near the bottom of the bank, I shouted, "A living glacier." These bent dirt lines show that the ice is flowing in its different parts with unequal velocity, and these embedded stones are journeying down to be built into the moraine, and they gradually become more abundant as they approach the moraine because there the motion is slower.

On traversing my new-found glacier, I came to a crevasse, down a wide and jagged portion of which I succeeded in making my way, and discovered that my so-called *snowbank* was clear green ice, and comparing the form of the basin which it occupied with similar adjacent basins that were empty, I was led to the opinion that this glacier was several hundred feet in depth.

Then I went to the "snowbanks" of Mounts Lyell and Maclure and believed that they also were true glaciers and that a dozen other snowbanks seen from the summit of Mount Lyell crouching in shadow were glaciers, living as any in the world and busily engaged in completing that vast work of mountain-making, accomplished by their giant relatives now dead, which, united and continuous, covered all the range from summit to sea like a sky.

John Muir

* * *

ARTICLE ON LIVING GLACIERS OF CALIFORNIA, 1875

I chose a camping ground for the night down on the brink of a glacier lake, where a thicket of Williamson spruce sheltered me from the night wind. After making a tin-cupful of tea, I sat by my campfire, reflecting on the grandeur and significance of the glacial records I had seen, and speculating on the developments of the morrow. As the night advanced, the mighty rocks of my mountain mansion seemed to come nearer. The starry sky stretched across from wall to wall like a ceiling and fitted closely down into all the spiky irregularities of the summits. After a long fireside rest and a glance at my field-notes, I cut a few pine tassels for a bed and fell into the clear death-like sleep that always comes to the tired mountaineer.

Early next morning I set out to trace the ancient ice current back to its farthest recesses, filled with that inexpressible joy experienced by every explorer in nature's untrodden wilds. The mountain voices were still as in the hush of evening; the wind scarce stirred the branches of the mountain pine; the sun was up, but it was yet too cold for the birds and marmots—only the stream, cascading from pool to pool, seemed wholly awake and doing. Yet the spirit of the opening, blooming day called to action.

I made excursions to the ice wombs situated on the head canyons of the Tuolumne and San Joaquin, and discovered that what at first sight and from a distance resemble extensive snowfields are really active glaciers, still grinding the rocks over which they flow.

That these residual glaciers are wearing the rocks on which they flow is shown by the fact that all the streams rushing out from beneath them are turbid with finely ground rock mud. They all present solid ice spouts creeping out from beneath their fountain snows, and all are carrying down stones that have fallen upon them, to be at length deposited in moraines.

In some transversal crevasses, as, for example, near the middle of the eastern branch of the Lyell Glacier, sections of blue ice eighty to a hundred feet deep occur, while the differential motion is manifested in the curves of the dirt bands and of the blue veins and moraines, not a single glacial attribute being either wanting or obscure. But notwithstanding the plainness and completeness of the proof, some of my friends who never take much trouble to investigate for themselves continued to regard my observations and deductions with distrust. I therefore determined to fix stakes in one of the more accessible of the glaciers, and measure their displacement, with a view to making the ordinary demonstration of true glacial movement. . . . The Maclure Glacier, situated on the north side of the mountain of that name, seemed best fitted for my purposes, and with the assistance of my friend Galen Clark, I planted five stakes in it on the 21st of August, 1872, guarding against their being melted out by sinking them to a depth of five feet. Four of them were extended across the glacier in a straight line, beginning on the east side about half-way between the head and foot of the glacier, and terminating near the middle of the current. Stake No. 1 was placed about 25 yards from the side of the glacier; No. 2, 94 yards; No. 3, one hundred and fifty-two yards; No. 4, 225 yards. No. 5 was placed up the glacier about midway between the *Bergschrund* and No. 4. On the 6th of October, or forty-six days after being planted, I found the displacement of stake No. 1 to be 11 inches, No. 2 to be 18 inches, No. 3 to be 34 inches, No. 4 to be 47 inches, and No. 5 to be 46 inches. As stake No. 4 was near the middle of the current, it was probably not far from the point of maximum velocity—47 inches in forty-six days, or about 1 inch per twenty-four hours.

A glacier is a current of ice derived from snow. Complete glaciers of the first order take their rise on the mountains and descend into the sea, just as all complete rivers of the first order do . . . but now the world is so warm and the snow crop so scanty, nearly all the glaciers left alive have melted to mere hints of their former selves. The Lyell Glacier is now less than a mile long; yet, setting out from the frontal moraine, we may trace its former course on grooved and polished surfaces and by immense canyons and moraines a distance of more than forty miles.

The main cause that has prevented the earlier discovery of Sierra Nevada glaciers is simply the want of explorations in the regions where they occur. The labors of the State Geological Survey in this connection amounted to a slight reconnaissance, while the common tourist, ascending the range only as far as Yosemite Valley, sees no portion of the true Alps containing the glaciers excepting a few peak clusters in the distance.

Excerpt from "Letter from John Muir to Jeanne C. Carr, Yosemite Valley, October 8, 1872," in John Muir, *Letters to a Friend: Written to Mrs. Ezra S. Carr, 1866–1879* (Boston: Houghton Mifflin, 1915), 132–38. Excerpt from John Muir, "Living Glaciers of California," *Harper's New Monthly Magazine* 51 (November 1875): 769–76.

FIRST EXPLORATION OF THE
SOUTHERN SIERRA

I N JUNE 1873, JOHN MUIR, then thirty-five, anticipated the arrival of his friend Jeanne Carr in Yosemite. Returning from an excursion to Mount Lyell with two young Englishmen, and having protected his face with a bark mask, Muir wrote to Carr requesting she bring green spectacles to protect his eyes from snow blindness. In an atmosphere Carr described as one in which they felt wedded to nature, she arrived at Mariposa Grove along with Albert Kellogg, noted botanist and founder of the California Academy of Science, and landscape painter William Keith. Carr carried with her the green spectacles Muir requested.[1]

Carr, Kellogg, Keith, and Muir traveled out of Yosemite Valley up into the Tuolumne River region, sliding over ice and snow on the glacier-polished rocks, creeping on hands and knees, barefooted and handed. Returning to Yosemite Valley on July 11, Muir led a group that included Keith; Keith's wife and son; and Emily Pelton, a friend from Prairie

du Chien, Wisconsin, up Mount Dana and down to Mono
Lake. Remaining in the Valley, Carr and Kellogg collected
plant specimens. Upon the return of Muir, the Keith family,
and Pelton, a third excursion out of the Valley included Muir,
Carr, Kellogg, a driver, and two packhorses carrying 150
pounds of provisions—enough for six weeks. Muir went on
alone for fourteen days with few provisions and no blankets.
In writing to his sister Sarah Muir Galloway, Muir noted that
the trip lasted over five weeks—with no mention of Carr
or Kellogg—and was the hardest he had undertaken in the
mountains.[2]

With the exception of Keith, his family, and Pelton, the
excursion party remained together until early September,
when Carr left Yosemite Valley and returned to Oakland,
California. Muir traveled out of the Valley with Kellogg;
Galen Clark, who left the excursion party two weeks into
the trip to return to Yosemite, where he served as guardian;
and Billy Simms, the shepherd Muir had accompanied in
1869 to Tuolumne Meadows. They arrived at Clark's Station
on September 13 and continued on into the southern Sierra,
the Kings River region, and Mount Whitney. Carr planned
to meet Muir and Kellogg at Lake Tahoe in late October
to continue exploring, but the death of her son, Ezra Smith
Carr, made it impossible for her to join them. He had been
crushed between two railroad cars in Alameda, California.
Leaving Tahoe City, Muir traveled to Oakland, where he

spent the end of the year writing a series of articles titled "Studies in the Sierra" for the *Overland Monthly* magazine.

* * *

JOURNAL ENTRIES, SEPTEMBER 26–OCTOBER 12, 1873

South Fork, San Joaquin. September 26. Night.

I am camped at the head of this San Joaquin Yosemite this ninth day, in a small oval dry lake-basin, with a rocky wall fifty feet above the river. The basin here is filled with fallen trees and fringed with willow. I set out this noon for the icy summits, leaving Clark, Billy, and Doctor Kellogg in camp on a moraine with the animals. I have a week's provisions.

This San Joaquin Canyon all the way up from the lowest to the highest yosemite is very rough. One is constantly compelled to ascend knobs and buttresses that rise sheer or steeply inclined from the water's edge. . . . The scenery from the first main fork is very grand. The walls are steep and close, fold on fold, rising to a height of three thousand to four thousand feet.

I saw a fine band of mountain sheep [Sierra Nevada bighorn sheep, *Ovis canadensis sierra*]. . . . They first had to cross loose angular blocks of granite, which they did splendidly; then they leaped up the face of the mountain just where I thought they wouldn't, and perhaps couldn't, go. I could have scaled the same precipice, but not where they did. I could have followed in most places only by being barefooted.

Looking at them I often cried out, "That was good!". . . I exulted in the power and sufficiency of Nature, and felt like saying aloud to God as to a man, "Well done!" Our horses roll end over end, and our much-vaunted mules, so surefooted and mountain-capable, roll like barrels. I must so often judge for my horse. . . . I know the slope he can bear and how he will be likely to come off in making various rock steps. . . . These noble fellows [the bighorn sheep]—I would like their company!

Camp on South Fork, San Joaquin. September 30.

In camp again with the main party. Up early and went with Clark to a point on the divide to view the landscape and plan the route. A vast wilderness of rocks and canyons. Clark groaned and went home.

Camp on divide between North and Middle Fork, Kings River. October 4.

Camped fifteen hundred feet above the river. . . . The view is lovely from this dark, rocky ridge nobly designed. . . . Before us lies the river canyon with innumerable folds and groves sweeping down to it in front, swell over swell, boss over boss, oak-dotted below, pine-feathered above.

Camped at Thomas Mills. Altitude fifty-seven hundred feet. October 6.

Coming here we had a long, weary uphill climb. Up from the valley over a hill five hundred feet, then down two thousand feet, to the wide-open, level-bottomed, oak-dotted valley of Mill Creek, past an Indian town, then up the valley six miles to a ranch and wagon road and six miles more to the mills. Beautiful valleys, brown as the plains.

October 7.

Sunrise, beams pouring through gaps in the rocky crest, warm level beams brushing across the shoulders in so fitting a way they seem to have worn channels for themselves as glaciers do.

Among the Big Trees. Altitude sixty-five hundred feet.

I saw a great many fine trees, fifteen to twenty-five feet in diameter, bulging moderately at the base, and holding their diameter in noble simplicity and symmetry. The "General Grant" is burned near the ground on the east side, and bulges in huge gnarly waves and crags on the north and west. Its bole above the base thirty or forty feet is smooth and round.

The grand old tree has been barbarously destroyed by visitors hacking off chips and engraving their names in all styles. Men residing in the grove, shingle-making, say that in the last six weeks as many as fifty visitors have been in the grove. It is easy of access by a wagon-road between Thomas Mills and the Big Trees.

The great Kings River Canyon is just a few days beyond, with all that is most sublime in the mountain scenery of America, and as the Southern Pacific Railroad is completed beyond Visalia, this whole region is now comparatively accessible to tourists.

The general appearance of the grove is so like that of Mariposa that one familiar with the latter grove can hardly know that this Kings River grove is not the Mariposa. I could not choose between the two.

At mouth of first tributary of South Fork Kings River. October 11.

Set out for Mount Tyndall alone, leaving Billy and Dr. Kellogg at camp with the animals.[3]

It is hard traveling along this portion of the stream, the avalanche material having been planted with poplars and all kind of chaparral. Even the bears seem at times to be at fault in making their trails.

At an elevation of ninety-seven hundred feet, the South Fork divides into many branches that run up to the glaciers and neves of a noble amphitheatre of lofty mountains, forming fountains for the brave young river.

I ascended two peaks in the afternoon. Clouds gathered about the brows, now dissolving, now thickening and shooting down into and filling up the canyons with wonderful rapidity. A great display of cloud motion about and above and beneath me.

Hurrying down from amid a thicket of stone spires to the tree-line and water, I reached both at dark. A grand mountain towers above my camp. A rushing stream brawls past its base. Willows are on one side, dwarf *flexilis* on the other. The moon is doing marvels in whitening the peaks with a pearly luster, as if each mountain contained a moon. I have leveled a little spot on the mountain-side where I may nap by my fireside. The altitude of my camp is eleven thousand five hundred feet, and I am blanketless.

October 12.

Set out early for Mount Tyndall and reached the summit about 9 a.m. Had grand views of the valley of the Kern and the Greenhorn Mountains and north and south along the axis of the range, and out over the Inyo Range and the Great Basin. Descended and pushed back to the main camp. Arrived about noon to find Billy and Dr. Kellogg gone, though they promised to wait three days for me. They left me neither horse nor provisions. I pushed on after them, following their tracks on the trail towards Kearsarge Pass, by long stretches of dry meadows and many lakes. . . . The pass is over twelve thousand feet high. *Primula suffrutescens* is abundant on the granite sand up to the head of the pass. The scenery of the summit is grand. *Pinus flexilis* abundant. I overtook the runaway train at sunset, a mile over the divide, just as they were looking for a camping-ground. When asked why they had left me, they said they feared I would not return. Strange that in the mountains people from cities should so surely lose their heads.

Excerpts from Muir's journals in John Muir, *John of the Mountains: The Unpublished Journals of John Muir,* ed. Linnie Marsh Wolfe (Boston: Houghton Mifflin, 1938), 176–86.

A SHASTA STORM

LEAVING TAHOE CITY IN NOVEMBER 1873, John Muir arrived in Oakland, California, at the home of J. B. McChesney and his wife, Sarah, friends of Jeanne Carr, who also resided in Oakland. Muir dressed casually with a sprig of greenery in his jacket pocket. He ate most meals in restaurants and developed a friendship with John Swett, who lived in San Francisco. A pioneer in California public education, Swett was also a friend of Jeanne. Beginning in November 1875, Muir would reside at the Swett residence. Muir stayed with the McChesneys to write a series of articles on a study of the geological formation and features of the Sierra Nevada for the *Overland Monthly* magazine. The first of the seven articles appeared in May 1874, and the final installment was published in January 1875.

With the series written, Muir left Oakland in September 1874 to return to Yosemite, though he felt he was a stranger in the Valley. In October he wrote to Jeanne that he escaped the civilization of Oakland and now, though Yosemite no longer felt like home, he believed he was hopelessly and forever a mountaineer, living "only to entice people to look at Nature's loveliness." A plan to be among the Sierra foothills and then travel northward was thwarted by the mountains that seized him, and he was up the Merced Canyon.[1]

In late October, Muir finally departed from Yosemite and traveled on foot, alone, north along the old California-Oregon stage road Shastaward, taking notes along the way for a series of articles he would write for the *San Francisco Daily Evening Bulletin.* From the stage coach inn and tavern Sisson's Station, in Siskiyou County, California, Muir wrote to Carr that icy Shasta was fifteen miles away. Preparing for his ascent of Mount Shasta, forewarned by locals that it was two months too late to climb, Muir noted that he liked snow, frost, and ice. He climbed, crept, and slid through deep snow to the summit, where he spent two hours. In an approaching storm, he retreated to camp, made a hollow "storm-nest," and snuggled beneath wool blankets with food for one week that would stretch to three if necessary. Covered in three inches of snow, in the wild wind, Muir watched bighorn sheep huddle under a pine. On the third day, though Muir had instructed he be left alone, Jerome Fay sent by Sisson arrived riding a horse and leading another. Reluctantly, Muir rode down the mountain.[2]

* * *

SISSON'S STATION, NOVEMBER 24, 1874

I followed the main Oregon and California stage-road from Redding to Sisson's, and besides trees, squirrels, and beautiful mountain-streams, I came upon some interesting men, rugged, weather-beaten fellows, who, in hunting and mining, had been brought face to face with many a Shasta storm. Most of them were a kind of almanacs, stored with curious facts and dates and ancient weather-notes, extending through a score of stormy mountain years. Whether the coming winter was to be mild or severe was the question of questions, and the diligence and fervor with which it was discussed was truly admirable. A picturesque series of prognostications were offered, based by many different methods upon the complexion of the sky, the fall of leaves, the flight of wild geese, etc., each of which seemed wholly satisfactory only to its author.

A pedestrian upon these mountain-roads is sure to excite curiosity, and many were the interrogations put concerning my little ramble. When told that I came from town for an airing and a walk, and that icy Shasta was my mark, I was invariably informed that I had come the wrong time of year. The snow was too deep, the wind too violent, and the danger of being lost in blinding drifts too great. And when I hinted that clean snow was beautiful, and that storms were not so bad as they were called, they closed the argument by directing attention to their superior experiences, declaring most emphatically that the ascent of "Shasta Butte" through the snow was impossible. Nevertheless, I watched the robins eating wild cherries and rejoiced in brooding over the miles of lavish snow that I was to meet. Sisson gave me bread and venison, and before noon of the 2d of November I was in the frosty azure of the summit.

In journeying up the valley of the Sacramento, one obtains frequent glimpses of Mount Shasta through the pine trees from the tops of hills and ridges, but at Sisson's there is a grand out-opening both of the mountains and the forests, and Shasta stands revealed at just the distance to be seen most comprehensively and impressively. It was in the middle of the last day of October that I first beheld this glorious picture. Gorgeous thickets of the thorn, cherry, birch, and alder flamed around the meadow. There were plenty of bees and golden-rods, and the warm air was calm as the bottom of a lake. Standing on the hotel-veranda and looking only at outlines, there, first of all, is a brown meadow with its crooked stream, then a zone of dark forest—its countless spires of fir and pine rising above one another, higher, higher in luxuriant ranks—and above all the great white Shasta cone sweeping far into the cloudless blue; meadow, forest, and mountain inseparably blended and framed in by the arching sky. I was in the heart of this beauty next day. Sisson, who is a capital mountaineer, fitted me out for calms or storms as only a mountaineer could, with a week's provisions so generous in kind and quantity it could easily be made to last a month in case of a fortunate snow-bound. Of course I knew the weariness of snow-climbing, and the stinging frosts, and the so-called dangers of mountaineering so late in the year; therefore I could not ask any guide to go with me. All I wanted was to have blankets and provisions deposited as far up in the timber as the snow would allow a packhorse to go. Here I could make a storm-nest and lie warm, and make raids up or around the mountain whenever the weather would allow. On setting out from Sisson's, my barometer as well as the sky gave notice of the approach of another storm, the wind sighed in the pines, filmy, half-transparent clouds began to dim the sunshine. It was one of those brooding days that [William] Keith so well knows how to paint, in which every tree of the forest and every mountain seems conscious of the approach of some great blessing and stands hushed and waiting.

The ordinary and proper way to ascend Shasta is to ride from Sisson's to the upper edge of the timber line—a distance of some eight or ten miles—the first day, and camp, and rising early push on to the summit, and return the second day. But the deep snow prevented the horses from reaching the camping-ground, and after stumbling and wallowing in the drifts and lava blocks, we were glad to camp as best we could, some eight or ten hundred feet lower. A pitch-pine fire speedily changed the climate and shed a blaze of light on the wild lava slope, and the straggling storm-bent pines around us. Melted snow answered for coffee-water, and we had plenty of delicious venison to roast.

Toward midnight I rolled myself in my blankets and slept until half-past one, when I arose and ate more venison, tied two days' provisions to my belt, and set out for the summit. After getting above the highest flexilis pines, it was fine practice pushing up the magnificent snow-slopes alone in the silence of the night. Half the sky was clouded; in the other half the stars sparkled icily in the thin, frosty air, while everywhere the glorious snow fell away from the summit of the cone in flowing folds more extensive and unbroken than any I had ever yet beheld. When the day dawned the clouds were crawling slowly and massing themselves, but gave no intimation of immediate danger. The snow was dry as meal and drifted freely, rolling over and over in angular fragments like sand or rising in the air like dust. The frost was intense, and the wind full of crystal dust, making breathing at times rather difficult. In pushing upward I frequently sank to my arm-pits between buried lava-blocks, but most of the way only to my knees. When tired of walking I still wallowed forward on all fours. The steepness of the slope—thirty-five degrees in many places—made any species of progress very fatiguing, but the sublime beauty of the snowy expanse and of the landscapes that began to rise around, and the intense purity of the icy azure overhead thrilled every fibre with wild enjoyment and rendered absolute exhaustion impossible. Yet I watched the sky with great caution, for it was easy to see that a storm was approaching. Mount Shasta rises ten thousand feet above the general level in blank exposure to the deep gulf-streams of air, and I have never been in a labyrinth of peaks and canyons where the dangers of a storm seemed so formidable as here. I was, therefore, in constant readiness to retreat into the timber. However, by half past ten o'clock I reached the utmost summit.

A succession of small storm-clouds struck against the summit pinnacles, like icebergs, darkening the air as they passed and producing a chill as definite and sudden as if ice-water were dashed in one's face. This is the kind of cloud in which snow-flowers grow, and I was compelled to begin a retreat, which, after spending a few minutes upon the main Shasta glacier and the side of the "Crater Butte," I accomplished more than an hour before dark, so that I had time to hollow a strip of ground for a nest in the lee of a block of red lava, where firewood was abundant.

Next morning, breaking suddenly out of profound sleep, my eyes opened upon one of the most sublime scenes I ever beheld. A boundless wilderness of storm-clouds of different age and ripeness were congregated over all the landscape for thousands of square miles, colored gray, and purple, and pearl and glowing white, among which I seemed to be floating, while the cone of Shasta above and the sky was tranquil and full of the sun. It seemed not so much an ocean as a land of clouds, undulating hill and dale, smooth purple plains, and silvery mountains of cumuli, range over range, nobly diversified with peaks and domes, with cool shadows between, and with here and there a wide trunk canyon, smooth and rounded, as if eroded by glaciers. I gazed enchanted, but cold gray masses drifting hither and thither . . . began to shut out the light, and it was evident that they would soon be marshalled for storm. I gathered as much wood as possible and snugged it shelteringly around my storm-nest. My blankets were arranged, and the topmost fastened down with stakes, and my precious bread-sack tucked in at my head, I was ready when the first flakes fell. All kinds of clouds began to fuse into one, the wind swept past in hissing floods, and the storm closed down on all things, producing a wild exhilaration.

My fire blazed bravely, I had a week's wood, a sack full of bread, and a nest that the wildest wind could not demolish, and I had, moreover, plenty of material for the making of snow-shoes if the depth of the snow should render them necessary.

The storm lasted about a week, and I had plenty to do listening to its tones and watching the gestures of the flexilis pine, and in catching snow crystals and examining them under a lens and observing the methods of their deposition as summer fountains.

On the third day Sisson sent up two horses for me, and his blankets, notwithstanding I had expressed a wish to be let alone in case it stormed. The horses succeeded in breaking through on the trail they made in coming up. In a few hours more this would have been impossible. The ride down through the forest of silver firs was truly enchanting, the thick flakes falling aslant the noble columns decorated with yellow lichen, and their rich, fronded branches drooped and laden in universal bloom. Farther down, the sugar pines with sublime gestures were feeding on the storm and waving their giant arms as if in ecstasy. At an elevation of four thousand feet above the sea, the snow became rain, and all the chaparral, cherry, manzanita, and ceanothus were bright and dripping.

The grand storm continues. The wind sings gloriously in the pine trees. Snow is still falling on icy Shasta, snow on snow, treasuring up food for forests and glaciers and for the thousand springs that gush out around its base.

Excerpt from John Muir, "Shasta in Winter. John Muir, the Geologist and Explorer, Ascends It. A Hard and Perilous Undertaking—Among the Glaciers, Lava-beds, and Storm-clouds. (Special Correspondence of the Bulletin.) Sisson's Station, November 24, 1874," *San Francisco Daily Evening Bulletin* (December 2, 1874): 1, col. 3.

SHASTA BEES

LEAVING SHASTA AND SISSON'S STATION, John Muir
traveled to Brownsville, Yuba County, California, on the
divide between the basins of the Yuba and Feather Rivers.
He remained there until January, exploring the adjacent
forests and mountains, continuing his observation of bighorn
sheep and enjoying the Shasta bees. The day after his arrival
in Brownsville, Muir pushed out into the woods in a wild
gale. With iron spikes driven into the soles of his shoes, he
climbed a one-hundred-foot Douglas fir to hear the varying
harmonics of its wind-filled topmost needles. Keeping his
lofty perch for hours as the tree arced, Muir thought about
the spectacle of the journey of life. "We all travel the milky
way together," he would later write of this experience, "trees
and men; but it never occurred to me until this storm-day,
while swinging in the wind, that trees are travelers in the
ordinary sense. They make many journeys, not extensive ones
. . . but our own little journeys, away and back again, are only
little more than tree-wavings."[1]

From Brownsville, on January 16, 1875, Muir wrote to

his sister Sarah that he had not in all his wanderings found a single person as free as himself. Bound to his studies as he was and to his own life with no feeling of haste, Muir noted that he would sit for hours in close observation of nature, looking into the faces of flowers and the bees he observed on the flanks of Mount Shasta. Swept onward, he left Shasta and returned to the McChesney home in Oakland, homesick for the mountains by late February.[2]

* * *

SISSON'S STATION, NEAR MOUNT SHASTA, DECEMBER 17, 1874

The Shasta woods are full of wild bees, and their honey is exactly delicious. At least such was the quality of my samples, and no wonder, inasmuch as it was in great part derived from the nectar bells of a huckleberry bog by bees that were let alone to follow their own sweet ways. The hive was a living pine tree, and the distance to the honey-bells was only a moment's buzz. Bees themselves could hardly hold the conception of a more honeyful place—honey-bog to left of them; honey-bog to right of them; blooming willows for springtime; golden-rods for autumn; and beside a'that and a'that, miles of acres of buttercups and columbines and rosy chaparral. Regarding Mount Shasta from a bee point of view and beginning at the summit, the first five thousand feet is clothed in summer with glaciers and rags of snow, and is, of course, almost entirely honeyless. The next one thousand feet of elevation is a brown zone tufted and matted with bush penstemon.... Next comes the silver-fir zone, about twenty-five hundred feet in height, containing few sweet flowers, but rich in honey-dew and pollen. Next the zone of honey-bearing chaparral or Shasta heather, forming the smooth, sunny slopes of the base. This last is six or seven miles wide and has a circumference of more than seventy miles. Companies of spruce and pine break across it in well-watered sections; yet, upon the whole, it is remarkably regular and contains all the principal honey-grounds of the mountain.

The formation of the Shasta bee lands is easily understood. Shasta is a fire mountain, created by a succession of eruptions of ashes and molten lava, which, pouring over the lips of the craters, layer over layer, grew outward and upward like a trunk of an exogenous tree. During the glacial period the whole Shasta cone was capped with ice, which by erosion degraded it to some extent and remodeled its flanks. When at length the glacial period began to draw near a close, the ice-cap was gradually melted off around the bottom, and in receding and breaking up into its present condition, deposited those irregular heaps and rings of moraine matter upon which the Shasta forests are growing. The glacial erosion of most of the Shasta lavas gives rise to soils composed of rough boulders of moderate size and a great deal of light, porous, sandy *detritus*, which yields very readily to the transporting power of running water. An immense quantity of this finer material was sorted out and washed down from the upper slopes of the mountain by an ancient flood of extraordinary magnitude, and redeposited in smooth, delta-like beds around the base. These form the main honey-grounds. The peculiar vegetation for which they were planned was gradually acquired, huckleberry bogs were planted, the seasons became summer, the chaparral became sweeter, until honey distills like dew. In this glorious honey zone, the Shasta bees rove and revel, clambering in bramble and huckle-bloom, ringing and singing, now down among buttercups, now out of sight in the rosy blossoms of the buckthorn. They consider the lilies and roll into them; and like lilies they toil not, for bees are run by sun-power, just as mill-wheels are by water-power, and when the one has plenty of water and the other plenty of sun, they hum and quiver alike.

I have often thought in bright, settled sun weather, that I could tell the time of day by the comparative energy of bee movements. Gentle and moderate in the cool of the morning, gradually increasing in fervor, and at high noon, thrilling and quivering in wild sun-ecstasy.

Bees are as directly the outcome of bright light as flowers are. Bee death and flower death are also alike—merely a sun-withering and evaporation.

Shasta bees appear to be better fed than any other I know of. They are dainty feeders and enormously cordial withal. Mint moths and humming-birds seldom set foot on a flower, but reach out and suck through long tubes as through straws; but bees hug and clasp and rub their blunt countenances upon them like round, awkward children upon their mothers.

Of all the overworked and defrauded toilers of California towns, only about twenty came to the daylight of Shasta last season. How the glories of this region have been so long unvoiced when the Oregon and California stage has run daily past for years on the very skirts of the great white cone, is a mystery. There is no daylight in towns, and the weary public ought to know that there is light here, and I for one clear my skirts from the respon-sibility of silence by shouting a cordial *come*. Come a beeing; huckleberry bogs in full bloom are glorious sights, and they bloom twice a year. The flowers are narrow-mouthed, purple bells that seem to have caught the tones of the alpen glow. Later, these blooms turn to berries, and the leaves to crimson petals. Here you may go with the bees. Conceive if you can the magnetism of brushing through the bushes with myriads of honey-bells ringing against your knees, and besides, no softness ever enjoyed by human foot is comparable with the softness of a bog. Come all who need rest and light bending and breaking with over work, leave your profits and losses and metallic dividends and come a beeing. It is hard to die the dark death of towns, hearse, coffin, cloth, and countenances all black. In June the base of Mount Shasta will be as white with honey bloom as the summit with snow. Follow the bees, and be showered with blossoms; take a baptism and a honey-bath and get some sweetness into your lives.

If you like to think, there is plenty here to think at. How Shasta fires have burned and builded, and how, notwithstanding it is still hot within, glaciers dwell on its flanks; and how as one of the grand ashy hearths of nature its base flows with honey. Geology, botany, zoology, grand object lessons in each, and if you like hunting there is game in abundance. But better let blood alone and come purely a beeing. The honey grounds will be blooming in June.

John Muir, "Shasta Bees. A Honeyful Region—The Bee Lands—A Summer Paradise. (From Our Special Correspondent.) Sisson's Station near Mt. Shasta, December 17, 1874," *San Francisco Daily Evening Bulletin,* January 5, 1875, 2, col. 5.

WILD WOOL

DURING THE SUMMER OF 1869, when John Muir trekked with 2,050 domestic sheep from the Sierra foothills up into the mountains and across to Tuolumne Meadows, he observed the destructive effect of the domestic sheep. Forever after, he referred to them as "hoofed locusts," as they left not a leaf or a root wherever they grazed. The experience would lead to Muir's future campaign to expel them from the Sierra and to create Yosemite National Park in 1890. In April 1875 he published his essay "Wild Wool," the result of his close observation of bighorn sheep during his trip to Mount Shasta in 1874. The wool of the wild sheep, composed of fine wool and coarse hair, exceeded in fineness the average grades of domestic sheep. Muir equated the fineness of wild sheep with the one great want of civilization—pure wildness, where for him resided freedom, hope, and truth.

* * *

Moral improvers have calls to preach. I have a friend who has a call to plow, and woe to the daisy sod or azalea thicket that falls under the savage redemption of his keen steel shares. Not content with the so-called subjugation of every terrestrial bog, rock, and moor-land, he would fain discover some method of reclamation applicable to the ocean and the sky that in due calendar time they might be made to bud and blossom as the rose. Our efforts are of no avail when we seek to turn his attention to wild roses, or to the fact that both ocean and sky are already about as rosy as possible—the one with stars, the other with dulse, and foam, and wild light. The practical developments of his culture are orchards and clover-fields that wear a smiling, benevolent aspect and are very excellent in their way, though a near view discloses something barbarous in them all. Wildness charms not my friend, charm it never so wisely; and whatsoever may be the character of his heaven, his earth seems only a chaos of agricultural possibilities calling for grubbing-hoes and manures.

Sometimes I venture to approach him with a plea for wildness, when he good-naturedly shakes a big mellow apple in my face, and reiterates his favorite aphorism: "Culture is an orchard apple; nature is a crab." All culture, however, is not equally destructive and inappreciative. Azure skies and crystal waters find loving recognition, and few there be who would welcome the axe among mountain pines or would care to apply any correction to the tones and costumes of mountain water-falls. Nevertheless, the barbarous notion is almost universally entertained by civilized men, that there is in all the manufactures of nature something essentially coarse which can and must be eradicated by human culture. I was, therefore, delighted in finding that the wild wool growing upon mountain sheep in the neighborhood of Mount Shasta was much finer than the average grades of cultivated wool. This *fine* discovery was made some three months ago, while hunting between Shasta and Lower Klamath Lake. Three fleeces were obtained—one that belonged to a large ram about four years old, another to a ewe about the same age, and another to a yearling lamb. After parting their beautiful wool on the side and many places along the back, shoulders, and hips, and examining it closely with my lens, I shouted: "Well done for wildness! Wild wool is finer than tame!"

My companions stooped down and examined the fleeces for themselves, pulling out tufts and ringlets, spinning them between their fingers, and measuring the length of the staple, each in turn paying tribute to wildness. It *was* finer, and no mistake, finer than Spanish Merino. Wild wool *is* finer than tame.

"Here," said I, "is an argument for fine wildness that needs no explanation. Not that such arguments are by any means rare, for all wildness is finer than tameness, but because fine wool is appreciable by everybody alike—from the most speculative president of national wool-growers' associations, all the way down to the humblest gude-wife spinning by her ingleside."

Nature is a good mother and sees well to the clothing of her many bairns—birds with smoothly imbricated feathers, beetles with shining jackets, and bears with shaggy furs. In the tropical south, where the sun warms like a fire, they are allowed to go thinly clad; but in the snowy north-land she takes care to clothe warmly. The squirrel has socks and mittens, and a tall broad enough for a blanket; the grouse is densely feathered down to the ends of his toes; and the wild sheep, besides his under-garment of fine wool, has a thick overcoat of hair that sheds off both the snow and the rain. Other provisions and adaptations in the dresses of animals, relating less to climate than to the more mechanical circumstances of life, are made with the same consummate skill that characterizes all the love–work of nature. Land, water, and air, jagged rocks, muddy ground, sand-beds, forests, underbrush, grassy plains, etc., are considered in all their possible combinations while the clothing of her beautiful wildlings is preparing. No matter what the circumstances of their lives may be, she never allows them to go dirty or ragged. The mole, living always in the dark and in the dirt, is yet as clean as the otter or the wave-washed seal; and our wild sheep, wading in snow, roaming through bushes, and leaping among jagged storm-beaten cliffs, wears a dress so exquisitely adapted to its mountain life that it is always found as unruffled and stainless as a bird.

On leaving the Shasta hunting-grounds, I selected a few specimen tufts and brought them away with a view to making more leisurely examinations; but, owing to the imperfectness of the instruments at my command, the results thus far obtained must be regarded only as rough approximations.

As already stated, the clothing of our wild sheep is composed of fine wool and coarse hair. The hairs are from about two to four inches long, mostly of a dull bluish-gray color, though varying somewhat with the seasons. In general characteristics, they are closely related to the hairs of the deer and antelope, being light, spongy, and elastic, with a highly polished surface, and though somewhat ridged and spiraled, like wool, they do not manifest the slightest tendency to felt or become taggy. A hair two and a half inches long, which is perhaps near the average length, will stretch about one-fourth of an inch before breaking. The diameter decreases rapidly both at the top and bottom, but is maintained throughout the greater portion of the length with a fair degree of regularity. The slender tapering point in which the hairs terminate is nearly black; but, owing to its fineness as compared with the main trunk, the quantity of blackness is not sufficient to greatly affect the general color. The number of hairs growing upon a square inch is about ten thousand; the number of wool fibres is about twenty-five thousand, or two and a half times that of the hairs. The wool fibres are white and glossy, and beautifully spiraled into ringlets. The average length of the staple is about an inch and a half. A fibre of this length, when growing undisturbed down among the hairs, measures about an inch; hence the degree of curliness may easily be inferred. I regret exceedingly that my instruments do not enable me to measure the diameter of the fibres, in order that their degrees of fineness might be definitely compared with each other and with the finest of the domestic breeds; but that the three wild fleeces under consideration are considerably finer than the average grades of Merino shipped from San Francisco is, I think, unquestionable.

When the fleece is parted and looked into with a good lens, the skin appears of a beautiful pale-yellow color, and the delicate wool fibres are seen growing up among the strong hairs, like grass among stalks of corn, every individual fibre being protected about as specially and effectively as if enclosed in a separate husk. Wild wool is too fine to stand by itself, the fibres being about as frail and invisible as the floating threads of spiders, while the hairs against which they lean stand erect like hazel wands; but, notwith-standing their great dissimilarity in size and appearance, the wool and hair are forms of the same thing, modified in just that way and to just that degree that renders them most perfectly subservient to the well-being of the sheep. Furthermore, it will be observed that these wild modifications are entirely distinct from those which are brought chancingly into existence through the accidents and caprices of culture; the former being inventions of God for the attainment of definite ends. Like the modifications of limbs—the fin for swimming, the wing for flying, the foot for walking—so the fine wool for warmth, the hair for additional warmth and to protect the wool, and both together for a fabric to wear well in mountain roughness and wash well in mountain storms.

The effects of human culture upon wild wool are analogous to those produced upon wild roses. In the one case there is an abnormal development of petals at the expense of the stamens, in the other an abnormal development of wool at the expense of the hair. Garden roses frequently exhibit stamens in which the transmutation to petals may be observed in various stages of accomplishment, and analogously, the fleeces of tame sheep occasionally contain a few wild hairs that are undergoing transmutation to wool. Even wild wool presents here and there a fibre that appears to be in a state of change. In the course of my examinations of the wild fleeces mentioned above, three fibres were found that were wool at one end and hair at the other. This, however, does not necessarily imply imperfection, or any process of change similar to that caused by human culture. Water-lilies contain parts variously developed into stamens at one end, petals at the other, as the constant and normal condition. These half-wool half-hair fibres may therefore subserve some fixed requirement essential to the perfection of the whole, or they may simply be the fine boundary lines where an exact balance between the wool and hair is attained.

I have been offering samples of mountain wool to my friends, demanding in return that the fineness of wildness be fairly recognized and confessed, but the returns are deplorably tame. The first question asked is, "Wild sheep, wild sheep, have you any wool?" while they peer curiously down among the hairs through lenses and spectacles. "Yes, wild sheep, you *have* wool; but Mary's lamb had more. In the name of use, how many wild sheep think you would be required to furnish wool sufficient for a pair of socks?" I endeavor to point out the irrelevancy of the latter question, arguing that wild wool was not made for men but for sheep, and that, however deficient as clothing for other animals, it is just the thing for the brave mountain-dweller that wears it. Plain, however, as all this appears, the quantity question rises again and again in all its commonplace tameness. To obtain a hearing on behalf of nature from any other stand-point than that of human use is almost impossible. Domestic flocks yield more flannel per sheep than the wild, therefore it is claimed that culture has improved upon wildness; and so it has as far as flannel is concerned, but all to the contrary as far as a sheep's dress is concerned. If every wild sheep inhabiting the Sierra were to put on tame wool, probably only a few would survive the dangers of a single season. With their fine limbs muffled and buried beneath a tangle of hairless wool, they would become short-winded and fall an easy prey to the strong mountain wolves. In descending precipices they would be thrown out of balance and killed, by their taggy wool catching upon sharp points of rocks. Disease would also be brought on by the dirt which always finds a lodgment in tame wool, and by the draggled and water-soaked condition into which it falls during stormy weather.

No dogma taught by the present civilization seems to form so insuperable an obstacle in the way of a right understanding of the relations which culture sustains to wildness, as that which declares that the world was made especially for the uses of men. Every animal, plant, and crystal controverts it in the plainest terms. Yet it is taught from century to century as something ever new and precious, and in the resulting darkness the enormous conceit is allowed to go unchallenged.

I have never yet happened upon a trace of evidence that seemed to show that any one animal was ever made for another as much as it was made for itself. Not that nature manifests any such thing as selfish isolation. In the making of every animal, the presence of every other animal has been recognized. Indeed, every atom in creation may be said to be acquainted with and married to every other, but with universal union there is a division sufficient in degree for the purposes of the most intense individuality; and no matter what may be the note which any creature forms in the song of existence, it is made first for itself, then more and more remotely for all the world and worlds.

Were it not for the exercise of individualizing cares on the part of nature, the universe would be felted together like a fleece of tame wool. We are governed more than we know, and most when we are wildest. Plants, animals, and stars are all kept in place, bridled along appointed ways, *with* one another, and *through the midst* of one another . . . wild wood and tame wool—wild sheep and tame sheep—are not properly comparable, nor are they in any correct sense to be considered as bearing any antagonism toward each other; they are different things, planned and accomplished for wholly different purposes.

A little pure wildness is the one great present want, both of men and sheep.

Excerpt from John Muir, "Wild Wool," *Overland Monthly* 14 (April 1875): 361–66.

ASCENT OF MOUNT WHITNEY

I N MID-OCTOBER 1873, in Independence, Inyo County,
California, John Muir left his friends Albert Kellogg and
Billy Simms, with whom he was exploring the southern
Sierra, and set out for the summit of what he believed was
Mount Whitney. He gained the summit of Mount Langley,
about fourteen thousand feet, early on October 15. With
Mount Whitney still five or six miles distant and five hundred feet higher, Muir set off to climb it the same day. In
shirt sleeves, without fire or food, in an icy wind storm, he
reached the base of Whitney near midnight and spent the
early morning hours climbing in the bitter cold. Five hundred
feet below the summit of Whitney, Muir danced, leaping in
the air, swinging his arms, and clapping his hands to keep
from freezing. Turning back without arriving at the summit,
he reached his horse and supplies hours later and returned to
Independence on the evening of October 17.

Departing on October 19, direct from the east side,
Muir hiked up a canyon opposite Lone Pine and reached the
summit of Whitney at 8 a.m. on October 21, 1873. Later,

he noted how quickly he had recovered from the tremendous exposure, proving that he could not be killed in such a manner. Given a summer, matches, and a sack of meal, Muir was certain he could climb every mountain in the region. He was in fact the first to ascend Mount Whitney by a direct approach from the east.

In July 1875, Muir started down the Sierra range into the southernmost sequoia belt, through the Kings River Valley, for a second ascent of Mount Whitney with a party of mountaineers that included George Bayley of San Francisco and Charles Washburn, a student at the University of California, Berkeley, with "Buckskin Bill" as mule driver.

* * *

Men ascend mountains as instinctively as squirrels ascend trees, and, of course, the climbing of Mount Whitney was a capital indulgence, apart from the enjoyment drawn from landscapes and scientific pursuits. We set out from the little village of Independence with plenty of excelsior determination, Bayley, . . . rejoicing in warwhoops, much to the wonderment of sober passers-by. The massive sun-beaten Sierra rose before us out of the gray sagebrush levels like one vast wall nine thousand feet high, adorned along the top with a multitude of peaks that seem to have been nicked out in all kinds of fanciful forms for the sake of beauty. Mount Whitney is one of those wall-top peaks.

With the exception of our one young student, our party were mountaineers, and we chose the eastern route. . . . On the first day we rode our mules some eighteen miles, through a fine, evenly-planted growth of sage-brush to the foot of the range, immediately west of Lone Pine. Here we "found a *man*," a whole-souled Welchman by the name of Thomas, with whom we camped for the night, and where all was made ready for an early start up the mountain next morning. Each carried a loaf of bread, a handful of tea and a tincup, and a block of beef about four inches in diameter . . . the whole compactly bundled in half a blanket, and carried by a strap passed over the shoulder.

The highway by which we ascended was constructed by an ancient glacier that drew its sources from the eastern flank of Mount Whitney and the adjacent summits, and poured its icy floods into Owens Valley, which during the glacial epoch was a sea of ice. Of this mighty, rock-crushing ice-river, scarce a vestige remains, and its channel is now occupied by a dashing crystal stream that kept us good company all the way to the summit. The day was warm, and many were the delicious lavings we enjoyed among its pools beneath the cooling shadows of its leafy border groves. The great declivity of the canyon gives rise to numerous rapids and cascades, along the edges of which, soil of sufficient depth for the best wild gardens and thickets cannot be made to lie; but small oval flats of rich alluvium occur between the rocky inclines, rising one above another in almost regular order like stairs. Here the alder and the birch grow close together in luxuriant masses, crossing their topmost branches above the streams, and weaving a bowery roof.

At an elevation of about eight thousand feet above the sea. . . . [f]or a distance of two or three miles above the head of this wild Yosemite, the ascent is rather steep and difficult because the canyon walls come sheer down in many places to the brink of the rushing stream, leaving no free margin for a walk.

The difficulties I encountered in forcing my way through this portion of the gorge during my first ascent caused me to scan the gaps and terraces of the south wall, with a view to avoiding the bottom of the gorge altogether. Coming to the conclusion that the thing was at least practicable, I led the party over a rough earthquake talus, beneath an overhanging cliff, and up an extremely steep and narrow gully to the edge of the main canyon wall.

Here occurred the only accident worth mentioning connected with the trip. Washburn, who climbs slowing, was soon a considerable distance in the rear, and I sat down at the head of the narrow gully to wait for him. Bayley soon came up somewhat breathless with exertion, and without thinking of consequences, loosened a big boulder that went bounding down the narrow lane with terrible energy, followed by a train of small stones and dust. Washburn was about a hundred feet below, and his destruction seemed inevitable, as he was hemmed in between two sheer walls not five feet apart. We shouted to give him warning, and listened breathlessly until his answering shout assured us of his escape. On coming up weary and nerve-shaken with fright, he reported that the dangerous mass shot immediately over him as he lay crouched in a slight hollow. Falling rocks, single or in avalanches, form the greatest of all the perils that beset the mountaineer among the summit peaks.

By noon we reached a genuine glacier meadow, where we disturbed a band of wild sheep that went bounding across the stream and up the precipitous rocks out of sight. We were now ten thousand feet above sea level . . . having passed in half a day from the torrid plains of Owens Valley to an Arctic climate.

Here we caught our first fair view of the jagged, storm-worn crest of

Mount Whitney, yet far above and beyond, looming gray and ruin-like from a multitude of shattered ridges and spires. Onward we pushed, unwearied, waking hosts of new echoes with shouts of emphatic excelsior. Along the green, plushy meadow, following its graceful margin curves, then up rugged slopes of gray boulders that had thundered from the shattered heights in an earthquake, then over smooth polished glacier pavements to the utmost limits of the timber line, and our first day's climbing was done.

Our elevation was now eleven thousand five hundred feet, and as the afternoon was less than half done, we had ample time to prepare beds, make tea, and gather a store of pitchy pine roots for our night fire. We chose the same camping ground I had selected two years before on the edge of a sedgy meadow enameled with buttercups and daises, near a waterfall and snowbank. . . . There were the withered pine tassels on which I had slept, and circling heap of stones built as a shelter from the down rushing night wind, and the remains of my wood-pile gathered in case of a sudden snow-storm. Each made his own tin cupful of tea, and dinner was speedily accomplished. Then bed-building was vigorously carried on, each selecting willow shoots, pine tassels, or withered grass with a zeal and naturalness whose sources must lie somewhere among our ancient grandfathers. . . . I have experimented with all kinds of plant pillows with especial reference to softness and fragrance, and here I was so happy as to invent a new one, composed of the leaves and flowers of the alpine dodecatheon [shooting star], elastic, fragrant, and truly beautiful. Here we rested as only mountain-eers can. The wind fell to soft whispers, keen spiky shadows stole over the meadow, and pale rosy light bathed the peaks, making a picture of Nature's repose that no words can ever describe. Darkness came, and the night wind began to flow like a deep and gentle river; the cascades nearby sounded all its notes with most impressive distinctness, and the sky glowed with living stars. Then came the moon, awakening the giant peaks that seemed to return her solemn gaze. The grand beauty of our chamber walls came out in wonderfully clear relief, white light and jet shadows revealing their wild fountain architecture, divested of all distracting details.

We rose early and were off in the first flush of dawn, passing first over a rounded ice-polished brow, then along the north shore of a glacier lake whose simple new-born beauty enchanted us all. It lay imbedded in the rocks like a dark blue green—a perfect mountain eye. Along its northern shore we sped joyously, inspired with the fresh unfolding beauties of the morning, leaping . . . over morainal embankments and slopes of crystalline gravel; every muscle in harmonious accord, thrilled and toned. . . . Speedily we meet the glances of another crystal lake, and of our dearest alpine flowers . . . the very angels of mountain flora. Now the sun rose, and filled the rocks with beamless spiritual light. . . . Above the second lake basin we found a long upcurving field of frozen snow, across which we scampered . . . leaping with excess of strength and rolling over and over on the clean snow-ground, like dogs.

We followed the snow nearly to its upper limit, where it leaned against the dividing axis of the range, placing our feet in hollows melted by radiated heat from stones shot down from the crumbling heights. To scale the dividing ridge in front was impossible, for it swept aloft in one colossal wave with a vertical shattered crest. We were therefore compelled to swerve to the north; then carefully picking our way from ledge to ledge, gained the summit about 8 a.m. There stood Mount Whitney now without a single ridge between; its spreading base within a stone's throw; its pointed, helmet-shaped summit two thousand feet above us. We gazed but a moment on the surrounding grandeur; the mighty granite battlements; the dark pine woods far below, and the glistening streams and lakes; then dashed adown the western slope into the valley of the Kern. On my first ascent I pushed direct to the summit up the north flank, but the memories of steep slopes of ice and snow over which I had to pick my way, holding on by small points of stones frozen more or less surely into the surface, where a single slip would result in death, made me determine that no one would ever be led by me through the same dangers. I therefore led around the north base of the mountain to the westward, much to Bayley's disgust, who declared that he could, or at least *would* follow wherever I was able to lead. Cautious Washburn wisely gave in his adhesion for the longer and safer route, and I remained firm in avoiding the dangerous ice slopes. We passed along the rocky shores of a lake whose surface was still (July 21st) covered with cakes of winter ice, around the edges of which the color of the water was a beautiful emerald green. Beyond the lake we gradually climbed higher, mounting in a spiral around the northwest shoulder of the mountain, crossing many a strong projecting buttress and fluting hollow, then bearing to the left urged our way directly to the summit. Higher, higher, we climbed with muscles in excellent noise, the landscape becoming more and more glorious as the wild Alps rose in the tranquil sky. Bayley followed closely, lamenting the absence of danger, whenever in this attenuated air he could command sufficient breath. Washburn seldom ventured to leap from rock to rock, but moved mostly on all fours, hugging projecting angles and boulders in a sprawled, outspread fashion, like a child clinging timidly to its mother, often calling for directions around this or that precipice, and careful never to look down for fear of giddiness, yet from first to last evincing a most admirable determination and persistence of the slow and sure kind. Shortly after 10 o'clock a.m. we gained the utmost summit—a fact duly announced by Bayley as soon as he was rested into a whooping condition and before any note was taken of the wilderness of landscapes by which we were zoned. Undemonstrative Washburn examined the records of antecedent visitors, then remarked with becoming satisfaction, "I'm the first and only student visitor to this highest land in North America."

This mountain was first ascended in the summer of 1873, by a party of farmers and stock raisers from Owens Valley, who were taking exercise. It was ascended a few weeks later by Clarence King, myself and a few others, and this summer by one party besides our own.

We left the summit about noon and swooped to the torrid plains before sundown, as if dropped out of the sky.

Excerpt from John Muir, "Mount Whitney. Its Ascent by John Muir, the Explorer and Geologist. Different Routes—The Ascent from the East—A Minor Yosemite—Glacier Meadows and Glacier Lakes—Glorious Views—Successive Ascents. (Special Correspondence of the Bulletin.) Independence, Inyo County, August 17, 1875," *San Francisco Daily Evening Bulletin* (August 24, 1875): 1, cols. 2–3.

HALF DOME

At the end of August 1875, John Muir again headed south into the southern Sierra to spend two and a half months in further survey of the sequoia belt. Persuaded to take along the small mule Brownie, Muir had the mule carry provisions and a pair of blankets. Returning to Yosemite in November, Muir climbed Half Dome, first scaled by George Anderson on October 12, 1875. He met Anderson the following year. Anderson's intention was to hew timber for a stairway, about eight hundred feet in length, with nearly a thousand steps, securely railed in on both sides, to the summit of the dome. Muir considered Half Dome to be one of the few inaccessible rocks in the Valley, and he discouraged "as much as possible every project for laddering the South Dome, believing it would be a fine thing to keep this garden untrodden." With the steps and rails a foregone conclusion, Muir advised everyone to make the ascent of Half Dome: "For not to mention the glorious circumference of landscapes seen from its summit, the joyous leafy valley outspread a mile below, and far beyond, alp, and forest, and rolling granite seas. On these vast aerial thrones one always receives lasting impressions of an utter isolation from all the known ways of the world, leaving the soul free to expand and blend with fountain nature, as if one had died and gone to another star."[1]

* * *

Yosemite Valley, November 10, 1875.

The Yosemite South Dome [Half Dome] is the noblest rock in the Sierra, and George Anderson, an indomitable Scotchman, has made a way to its summit. . . . With the exception of the conoidal summit of Mount Starr King, and a few minor spires and pinnacles, the South Dome is the only inaccessible rock of the valley, and its inaccessibility is pronounced in very severe and simple terms, leaving no trace of hope for the climber without artificial means. But longing eyes were nonetheless fixed on its noble brow, and the Anderson way will be eagerly ascended.

John Conway, a resident of the valley, has a flock of small boys who climb smooth rocks like lizards, and some two years ago he sent them up the dome with a rope, hoping they might be able to fasten it with spikes driven into fissures, and thus reach the top. They took the rope in tow and succeeded in making it fast two or three hundred feet above the point ordinarily reached, but finding the upper portion of the curve impracticable without laboriously drilling into the rock, he called down his lizards, thinking himself fortunate in effecting a safe retreat.

Mr. Anderson began with Conway's old rope, part of which still remains in place, and resolutely drilled his way to the top, inserting eyebolts five or six feet apart, and making his rope fast to each in succession, resting his foot on the last bolt while he drilled for the next above. Occasionally some irregularity in the curve or slight foothold would enable him to climb fifteen or twenty feet independently of the rope, which he would pass and begin drilling again, the whole being accomplished in a few days. From this slender beginning he will now proceed to construct a substantial stairway which he hopes to complete in time for next year's travel; and as he is a man of rare energy, the thing will surely be done. Then, all may sing "Excelsior" in perfect safety.

On my return to the valley the other day, I immediately hastened to the Dome, not only for the pure pleasure of climbing in view, but to see what else I might enjoy and learn. Our first winter storm had bloomed, and all the mountains were mantled in fresh snow. I was therefore a little apprehensive of danger from the slipperiness of the rock, Anderson himself refusing to believe that any one could climb his rope in the condition it was then in. Moreover, the sky was overcast, and solemn snow-clouds began to curl and wreath themselves around the summit of the Dome, and my late experiences on icy Shasta came to mind. But reflecting that I had matches in my pocket and that a little firewood might be found, I concluded that in case of a dark storm the night could be spent on the Dome without suffering anything worth caring for. I therefore pushed up alone and gained the top without the slightest difficulty. My first view was perfectly glorious. A massive cloud of a pure pearl luster was arched across the valley, from wall to wall, the one end resting upon El Capitan, the other on Cathedral Rocks, the brown meadows shadowed beneath, with short reaches of the river shimmering in changeful light. Then, as I stood on the tremendous verge overlooking Mirror Lake, a flock of smaller clouds, white as snow, came swiftly from the north, trailing over the dark forests, and arriving on the brink of the valley descended with godlike gestures through Indian Canyon and over the Arches and North Dome, moving rapidly, yet with perfect deliberation. On they came, nearer, nearer, beneath my feet, gathering and massing, and filling the Tenaya abyss. Then the sun shone free, lighting them through and through and painting them with the splendors of the rainbow. It was one of those brooding days that come just between Indian summer and winter, when the clouds are like living creatures. Now and then the valley appeared all bright and cloudless, with its crystal river meandering through colored meadow and grove, while to the eastward the snowy peaks rose in glorious array, keenly outlined on the pure azure. Then, the clouds would come again, wreathing the Dome, and making a darkness like night.

Excerpt from John Muir, "South Dome, Its Ascent by George Anderson and John Muir—Hard Climbing but a Glorious View—Botany of the Dome—Yosemite in Late Autumn. (From Our Special Correspondent.) Yosemite Valley, November 10, 1875," *San Francisco Daily Evening Bulletin* (November 18, 1875): 1, col. 1.

A BATH

During a trip to Utah in May 1877, John Muir climbed in the Wasatch Mountains, traced ancient glacial rivers, and studied the wildflowers that carpeted the foothills and the shores of the Great Salt Lake. As a special correspondent for the *San Francisco Daily Evening Bulletin,* he recorded his observations and experiences, dashing into the Great Salt Lake and dipping his soul into the pines and firs, amid the wind waves of the mountains.

* * *

LAKE POINT, UTAH, MAY 20, 1877

When the north wind blows, bathing in Salt Lake is a glorious baptism, for then it is all wildly awake with waves, blooming like a prairie in snowy crystal foam. Plunging confidently into the midst of the grand uproar you are hugged and welcomed, and swim without effort, rocking and whirling up and down, round and round in delightful rhythm, while the winds sing in chorus, and the cool fragrant brine searches every fibre of your body, and at the end of your excursion you are tossed ashore with a glad God-speed, braced and salted and clean as a saint. The nearest point on the shore line is distant about ten miles from Salt Lake City, and is almost inaccessible on account of the boggy character of the ground, but by taking the Western Utah Railroad at a distance of twenty miles, you reach what is called Lake Point where the shore is gravelly and wholesome, and abounds in fine retreating bays that seem to have been made on purpose for bathing. Here the northern peaks of the Oquirrh range plant their feet in the clear blue brine, with the curving insteps, leaving no space for muddy levels. The crystal brightness of the water, the wild flowers and lovely mountain scenery make this a favorite summer resort for pleasure and health seekers. . . . But at the time of my first visit in May, I fortunately found myself alone. The hotel and bathhouse, which form the chief improvements of the place, were asleep in winter silence notwithstanding the year was in full bloom. It was one of those genial sundays when flowers and flies come thronging to the light, and birds sing their best. The mountain ranges, stretching majestically north and south, were piled with pearly cumuli, the sky overhead was pure azure, and the wind-swept lake was all aroll and aroar with white caps. I sauntered along the shore until I came to a sequestered cove, where buttercups and wild peas were blooming close down to the limit reached by the waves. Here, I thought, is just the place for a bath; but the breakers seemed terribly boisterous and forbidding as they came rolling up the beach, or dashed white against the black rocks that bounded the cove on the east. The outer ranks, ever broken, ever builded, formed a magnificent rampart, sculptured and corniced like the hanging wall of a bergschrund, appearing hopelessly insurmountable, however easily one might ride the swelling waves beyond. I feasted awhile on their surpassing beauty, watching their coming in from afar like faithful messengers, to tell their stories one by one; then I turned reluctantly away, to botanize and wait a calm. But the calm did not come that day, nor did I wait long. In an hour or two I was back again to the same little cove. The waves still sang the old storm song and rose in high crystal walls, seemingly hard enough to be cut in angular sections, like ice.

Without any definite determination I found myself undressed, as if someone else had taken me in hand; and while one of the largest waves was ringing out its message and spending itself on the beach, I ran out with open arms to the next and received a hearty salute. Then I was fairly launched and at home, tossed into right lusty relationship with the brave old lake. Away I sped in free, glad motion, as if, like a fish, I had been afloat all my life, now low out of sight in the smooth, glassy valleys, now bounding aloft on firm combing crests, while the crystal foam beat against my breast with keen, crisp clashing, as if composed of pure, crisp salt. I bowed to every wave, and each lifted me right royally to their shoulders, almost setting me erect on my feet, while they went speeding by like living creatures, blooming and rejoicing in the brightness of the day, and chanting the history of their grand old mountain home.

A good deal of nonsense has been written concerning the difficulty of swimming in this heavy water. "One's head would go down, and heels come up, and the acrid brine would burn like fire." I was conscious only of a joyous exhilaration, my limbs seemingly heeding their own business, without any discomfort or confusion; so much so, that without previous knowledge my experience on this occasion would not have led me to detect anything peculiar. In calm weather, however, the sustaining power of the water might probably be more marked. This was by far the most exciting and effective wave excursion I ever made this side the Rocky Mountains; and when at its close I was heaved ashore among the sunny grasses and flowers, I found myself a new creature indeed and went bounding along the beach . . . reinforced by the best life-salts of the mountains and ready for any race.

Excerpt from John Muir, "Notes From Utah. John Muir the Naturalist, on Bathing in Salt Lake—A Glorious Swim—Erroneous Impressions Corrected, (Special Correspondent of the Bulletin.) Lake Point, Utah, May 20, 1877," *San Francisco Daily Evening Bulletin* (June 14, 1877): 1, col. 1.

WATER OUZEL

IN RESIDENCE WITH THE John and Mary Swett family in San Francisco beginning in November 1875, John Muir had intended to write for publication. But at 1419 Taylor Street, in company with the four Swett children (Emily, Frank, Jack, and Helen), he had every opportunity to do what he most enjoyed: tell stories. The children often refused to go to bed until gathered by the fireplace to hear one of Muir's yarns. With a built-in audience, the stories he told became the source for articles. The success of "The Hummingbird of the California Waterfalls," about the life of the water ouzel, referred to as the American dipper, was written for *Scribner's Monthly* magazine in February 1878. This resulted in a request for additional manuscripts from the editorial staff, among them the conservationist Robert Underwood Johnson. Muir's descriptions of the western wilderness, of water ouzels, deer, marmots, and the Douglas squirrel, along with snowscapes and windstorms, impressed the nature-lover Johnson. Their collegial friendship would result in the collaborative effort to create Yosemite National Park in 1890.

For Muir, the hope of the world resided in wildness. The wildness of which he spoke and wrote dwelt in plants and mountains and in equal measure in the heartbeat of every creature that shares our journey around the earth as we travel through the universe. About his particular affection and reverence for our earth-born companions, Muir wrote: "How many hearts with warm red blood in them are beating under cover of the woods, and how many teeth and eyes are shining! A multitude of animal people, intimately related to us, but of whose lives we know almost nothing, are as busy about their own affairs as we are about ours."[1]

* * *

The waterfalls of the Sierra Nevada are frequented by only one bird, the ouzel or water-thrush (*Cinclus Mexicanus*, Sw.). He is a singularly joyous and lovable little fellow, about the size of a robin, clad in a plain water-proof suit of a blackish, bluish gray, with a tinge of chocolate on the head and shoulders. In form he is about as smoothly plump and compact as a pot-hole pebble; the flowing contour of his body being interrupted only by his strong feet and bill, and the crisp wing-tips, and up-slanted wrenish tail.

Among all the countless waterfalls I have met in the course of eight years' explorations in the Sierra, whether in the icy Alps or warm foothills or in the profound Yosemite canyons of the middle region, not one was found without its ouzel. No canyon is too cold for him, none too lonely, provided it be rich in white falling water. Find a fall or cascade or rushing rapid, anywhere upon a clear crystalline stream, and there you will surely find its complementary ouzel, flitting about in the spray, diving in foaming eddies, whirling like a leaf among beaten foam-bells, ever vigorous and enthusiastic, yet self-contained, and neither seeking nor shunning your company.

If disturbed while dipping about in the margin shallows, he either sets off with a rapid whir to some other feeding-ground up or down the stream, or alights on some half-submerged rock or snag out in the foaming current, and immediately begins to nod and courtesy like a wren, turning his head from side to side and performing many other odd dainty manners as if he had been trained at some bird dancing-school.

He is the mountain streams' own darling—the hummingbird of blooming waters, loving rocky ripple-slopes and sheets of foam as a bee loves flowers—as a lark loves sunshine and meadows. Among all the mountain birds, none has cheered me so much in my lonely wanderings—none so unfailingly. For winter and summer he sings, independent alike of sunshine and love, requiring no other inspiration than the stream on which he dwells. While water sings, so must he; in heat or cold, calm or storm, ever attuning his voice in sure accord, low in the drouth of summer and drouth of winter, but never silent.

One wild winter morning when Yosemite Valley was swept from west to east by a cordial snowstorm, I sallied forth to see what I might learn and enjoy. A sort of gray, gloaming-like darkness was kept up by the storm, and the loudest booming of the falls was at times buried beneath its sublime roar. The snow was already over five feet deep on the meadows, making very extended walks impossible without the aid of snow-shoes. I found no great difficulty, however, in making my way to a certain ripple on the river where one of my ouzels lived. He was at home as usual, gleaning his breakfast among the pebbles of a shallow portion of the margin, and apparently altogether unconscious of anything extraordinary in the weather. Presently he flew out to a stone against which the icy current was beating, and turning his back to the wind, sang delightfully as a lark in springtime.

What may be regarded as the separate songs of the ouzel are exceedingly difficult of description because they are so variable and at the same time so confluent. I have been acquainted with my favorite for eight years, and though, during most of this time I have heard him sing nearly every day, I still detect notes and strains that are quite new to me. Nearly all of his music is very sweet and tender, lapsing from his round breast like water over the smooth lip of a pool, then breaking farther on into a rich sparkling foam of melodious notes, which glow with subdued enthusiasm, yet without expressing much of the strong, gushing ecstasy of the bobolink or sky-lark.

His food consists of all kinds of water insects, which in summer are chiefly procured along shallow margins. Here he wades about, ducking his head under water and deftly turning over pebbles and fallen leaves with his bill, seldom choosing to go into deep water where he has to use his wings in diving.

He seems to be especially fond of the larvae of mosquitoes, found in great quantities attached to the bottom of smooth rock channels where the current is swift and shallow. When feeding in such places he wades upstream, and oftentimes while his head is under water the swift current is deflected upward along the glossy curves of his neck and shoulders, in the form of a clear, crystalline shell, which fairly encloses him like a bell-glass, the shell being constantly broken and re-formed as he lifts and dips his head; while ever and anon he sidles out to where the too powerful current carries him off his feet, and sweeps him rapidly down-stream; then he dexterously rises on the wing and goes gleaning again in shallower places.

They seldom swim more than a few yards on the surface, for, not being web-footed, they make rather slow progress, but by means of their strong, crisp wings they swim, or rather fly, with great celerity under the surface, often to considerable distances.

But it is in withstanding the force of rushing torrents that their strength of wing in this respect is most strikingly manifested. The following may be regarded as a fair illustration of their easy, unconscious powers of sub-aquatic flight. One winter morning, when the Merced River was blue and green with unmelted snow, I observed one of my ouzels perched on a snag out in the midst of a swift rushing rapid. He sang cheerily, as if everything was just to his mind, and while I stood on the bank admiring him, he suddenly plunged into the sludgy current, leaving his song broken abruptly off. After feeding a minute or two at the bottom, and when one would suppose he must inevitably be swept far down-stream, he emerged just where he went down, alighted on the same snag, showered the water beads from his feathers, and at once continued his unfinished song, splicing it together as if it had suffered no interruption.

The ouzel's nest is one of the most extraordinary pieces of bird architecture I ever beheld, so odd and novel in design, and so perfectly fresh and beautiful, and in every way so fully worthy of the genius of the little builder. It is about a foot in diameter, round and bossy in outline, with a neatly arched opening near the bottom, somewhat like an old-fashioned brick oven. It is built almost exclusively of green and yellow mosses, chiefly the beautiful fronded hypnum that covers the rocks and old drift-logs in the vicinity of waterfalls. These are deftly interwoven and felted together into a charming little hut, and so situated that many of the outer mosses continue to flourish as if they had not been plucked. A few fine, silky-stemmed grasses are occasionally found interwoven with the mosses, but with the exception of a thin layer lining the floor, their presence seems accidental, as they are of a species found growing with the mosses and are probably plucked with them. The site chosen for this curious mansion is usually some little rock-shelf within reach of the spray of a waterfall, so that its walls are kept green and growing, at least during the time of high water.

In these moss huts are laid, three or four eggs—white, like foam bubbles—and well may the little ouzels hatched from them, sing water songs, for they hear them all their lives, and even before they are born.

I have oftentimes observed the young just out of the nest making their odd gestures and seeming in every way as much at home as their experienced parents—like young bees in their first excursions to the flower fields. No amount of familiarity with people and their ways seems to change them in the least. To all appearances, their behavior is just the same on seeing a man for the first time as when seeing him every day.

Such, then, is the life of our little cinclus, beloved of every one who is so happy as to know him. Tracing on strong wing every curve of the most precipitous torrent, from one extremity of the California Alps to the other; not fearing to follow them through their darkest gorges and coldest snow-tunnels; acquainted with every waterfall, echoing their divine music; and throughout the whole of their beautiful lives interpreting all that we in our unbelief call terrible in the utterances of torrents, as only varied expressions of God's eternal love.

Excerpt from John Muir, "The Humming-Bird of the California Water-Falls," *Scribner's Monthly* 15 (February 1878): 545–54.

TAHOE IN WINTER

FOLLOWING HIS TRIP TO UTAH in May 1877, John Muir returned to southern California, spent five days in the San Gabriel Mountains, traveled on to the coast to the Santa Cruz Mountains to see the *Sequoia sempervirens* (the coastal Redwoods), and headed back to San Francisco. The Swett home at 1419 Taylor Street continued to provide him a safe haven.

A trip in September to Mount Shasta with Asa Gray, professor of botany at Harvard University, and Sir Joseph Hooker, British botanist and curator of the Kew Botanical Gardens, London, included a stop at Rancho Chico on the Sacramento River. There, the California pioneer General John Bidwell, his wife, Annie Kennedy Bidwell, and her sister, Sallie Kennedy, joined the excursion party to Mount Shasta. Following the departure of Gray and Hooker, the Bidwell party and Muir continued on to Mount Lassen. Upon their return to Rancho Chico, Bidwell had a skiff built for Muir. Christened *Spoonbill,* it was soon renamed by Muir, *Snagjumper,* as a result of its efficiency in surmounting snags. Muir floated down the Sacramento River to Sacramento, where he boarded a train to Visalia and headed for the Middle Fork of the Kings River with a young explorer, John Rigby. At Hopeton on the Merced River, Muir built a skiff, *Snagjumper II*, and drifted down the Merced River to the San Joaquin River and across the delta to Suisun Bay, a shallow tidal estuary, a northeastern extension of the San Francisco Bay, a total of 250 miles, to the town of Martinez, northeast of San Francisco.

A chance meeting of the Strentzel family and Muir at the home of Jeanne Carr in Oakland, California, during the summer of 1874, may have lessened the shock of his appearance on November 27, 1877, when wearing a faded greenish-hued coat worn at the elbows and wrists, with hair hanging down nearly to his shoulders, he arrived at the Strentzel ranch in the Alhambra Valley, California. He had walked the two miles from Martinez. Louie was twenty-seven when she first met Muir, then thirty-six. After their first meeting, Carr made every effort to arrange meetings between Muir and Louie to no avail. In March 1878, to escape the arduous nature of writing, Muir spent a week at Lake Tahoe, where he rolled in snow, swam in crystal water, sported in snowshoes [skis], and weathered in the winter beauty, "under all kinds of light, from the full white glow of clear noonday sunshine to the gray darkness of cordial snowstorms." Muir wrote to his friend Annie Kennedy Bidwell: "The whole was deliciously exhilarating, and I come back to this dull pen-life fairlit awakened and sane." There was never-ending pen work piling up against him.[1]

* * *

Californians are not so much as half conscious of the winter glory of the Sierra. We admire descriptions of the Swiss Alps, reading with breathless interest how the ice and snow load their sublime heights, and booming avalanches sweep their crowded forests; while our own Alps, grand as they, loom unnoticed along our eastern horizon. True, only mountaineers may penetrate their snow-blocked fastnesses to behold them in all their grandeur; but many of the sub-alpine valleys and inner basins remain open and approachable to every healthy man and woman, and even to children, all through the winter. In company with a friend and his two little sons, I have just returned from a week of weathering around Tahoe, where we had glorious views of winter, besides the enjoyment of a fine reviving roll in the snow, a swim in the icy lake, and some rich, lusty exercise on snow-shoes. All the weather was delightfully bracing and exhilarating, though varying rapidly almost from hour to hour   snowing, blowing, clear, and cloudy, but never rigorously cold.

The whole winter I am told has thus far been a remarkably mild one — the mildest since the region was settled — the mercury seldom making a very near approach to zero, even during the coldest nights, while the average noonday temperature was considerably above the freezing point.

The snow lies deep on the mountains and all round the shores, excepting only a few of the steeper sun-touched promontories; not so deep, however, as from the rainfall here one would be led to expect; but the canyons and woods and all the upper glacial fountains are well-filled, assuring abundance of summer water for the lakes and streams.

The greater portion of the snow deposited around the lofty summits of the range falls in small, crisp flakes and broken crystals; or, when accompanied by strong winds at a low temperature, the crystals instead of being locked together in their fall to form tufted flakes, are beaten and broken into meal and fine dust. But down in the forested region about the elevation of Lake Tahoe, the greater portion comes gently to the ground, light and feathery, some of the flakes nearly an inch in diameter, and is evenly distributed and kept from drifting to any great extent beneath the shelter of the trees. Every tree is loaded with this fairy bloom, bending down the branches, and hushing every leaf. When the storm is over and the sun shines, the snow at once begins to shift and settle and fall off in miniature avalanches, leaving the forest green again.

I have met but very few Californians even who have any adequate conception of the marvelous abundance of glacier lakes hidden away in the fastnesses of our mountains. . . . Lake Tahoe is King of them all, not only in size, but in surpassing beauty of its shores and waters. It seems a kind of heaven to which all the dead lakes of the lowlands had come with their best beauty spiritualized. It lies embosomed in lofty mountains near the northern extremity of the Alpine portion of the range, between the main axis and a spur that puts out on the east from near the head of Carson river, and, though twenty-one miles long by ten wide, and from about five hundred to sixteen hundred feet in depth, its basin was filled during the glacial period from the bottom to a point high above the present water level with solid ice, which, lavishly fed by the snows that fell on its mountain fountains, crawled slowly like a mighty river over the north . . . rim of the basin, crushing and grinding the mountains that lay in its way; and it was only at the close of the ice period that this noble lake, at least in anything like its present form, came into existence.

Excepting the forests that have sprung up around its shores, the post-glacial changes that have taken place are scarcely appreciable. The sediments carried forward by the overflowing streams have given rise to a few square miles of meadow land at the head of the lake, and the breaking through of a moraine dam three miles down the outlet has lowered the lake considerably, leaving shore benches, and lines on the rock promontories to mark the original level. But with these comparatively faint exceptions, the lake itself and all its compassing mountains, exist today in just about the condition they presented when first they came to light, on the removal of the ice mantle.

In this letter I intended only to say a good word for winter in the mountains, hoping to incite lovers of wild beauty to come and see, giving a sketch of my own excursion as an illustration of the ease and comfort with which such winter rambles may be made, but I have written too much, I fear, about the snow to leave room for more than the thinnest outline. We went by rail to Carson and set out thence by stage from Glenbrook. After ascending on wheels until we reached the snow line, the driver attached his four horses to a sled, hoping thus to cross the summit without great difficulty, but the mild weather had softened the snow, causing the horses to sink deeply and fall. The driver urged them on, however, until they had fallen a hundred times or so, and at length lay on their back dripping and reeking with their feet in the air, when, having made only about a mile in three hours, we abandoned the wrecked "outfit" and made our way over to the lake on foot. Next day we crossed to McKenny's on the west shore by the mail-boat, where we were at home. Here we spent a few long, delightful, health-giving days, rowing and bathing, racing at lightning speed down a mountain slope back of the house on snowshoes, and slipping about through the solemn, silent woods. Only the eldest of my companions ventured with me upon the steep mountain side. This was his first experience on snow-shoes, and the several descents he made were the most remarkable specimens of locomotion that I ever had the fortune to witness. In shooting down steep declivities, the long shoes should be kept strictly parallel, and every limb immovably braced. My friend, however, launched himself in wild abandon, limbs and shoes in chaotic entanglement—now in snow, now in air, whirling over and over in rolls and somersaults that would shame the most extravagant performances of a circus acrobat. How truly original and inimitable he was. It was all-refreshing, however, this downright contact with snow and sky; and on coming to rest with his runaway members deeply imbedded and far divorced, he would quietly gather himself, pick out the snow from his neck and ears, and say with preternatural solemnity, "This, Muir, is the poetry of motion."

We spent some rare evenings, too, in McKenney's old cabin, standing among the firs, banked in snow, but snug within.... Two live coons frolic on the floor, our grand old host smiling benignly and playing with them, the fire light on his weathered face. How big he seems thus relieved, and what a shadow he casts! The great, rousing, fragrant fire is the very god of the home.... A fine place this to forget weariness and wrongs and bad business.

We sailed to Tahoe City through a thick snowfall and completed our fine excursion by slipping down the Truckee valley on snowshoes.

Excerpt from John Muir, "Tahoe in Winter. John Muir Gives Some Curious Facts About Sierra Snow—Stored Up Snow Masses—Glacial Lakes—Snow Shoe Experiences—A Retired Hunter. (Correspondence of the Bulletin.)," *San Francisco Daily Evening Bulletin* (April 3, 1878): 4, cols. 1–2.

HERALD ISLAND

URING THE SPRING OF 1878, John Muir frequently
left the home of John and Mary Swett in San Francisco to visit the Strentzel ranch and Louie. His purpose
in visiting the ranch, he claimed, was discussions with her
father, a doctor, scientist, and experimental agriculturist
whose orchards and vineyards covered 856 acres, with an
extended estate of 2,665 acres. For the first time, in April
1879, Muir wrote to Louie and from her he received a gift
of flowers. "An orchard in a band box," he wrote. Betrothed
that spring, the following day Muir departed on his first trip
to Alaska. The Strentzels would not see him until February
1880, in time for the wedding in April. In the rolling hills
of the Alhambra Valley, at the home of her parents, Dr. John
and Louisiana Strentzel, amid a rainstorm, surrounded by
flowers gathered from the family ranch, Louie Wanda Strentzel, thirty-two, and John Muir, forty-one, were married on
April 14, 1880. After the wedding Muir returned to Alaska.[1]

In 1881, following the birth of their daughter Annie
Wanda in March, with the encouragement of Louie, Muir

accepted an invitation to join Captain Calvin L. Hooper, a friend who lived in Oakland, California. Although he was reluctant to leave, Muir joined the expedition on the *Corwin* that was searching for the lost steamer *Jeannette*, a naval exploration vessel that had taken an ill-fated voyage to the Arctic in 1879. This, Muir's third trip to Alaska, included an extended voyage to northwestern Alaska and islands in the Bering Sea and Arctic Ocean, as well as the shores of northeastern Siberia. It was an opportunity to explore regions he had not seen. Muir studied glaciation and flora during the six-month excursion from May through October 1881. One of the memorable experiences he recorded was the time spent on Herald Island, a Russian island in the Chukchi Sea, forty-three miles east of Wrangell Island. There, the crew hoped to find evidence left by the *Jeannette*, but they found nothing. Well after midnight in the arctic sunshine, Muir remained on the island in absolute silence on an immeasurable landscape.

* * *

Corwin (Off Herald Island), Arctic Ocean, July 31, 1881.

On the evening of the 30th [of July] we reached Herald Island, having been favored with delightful weather all the way, the ocean being calm and glassy as a mountain lake, the surface stirred gently here and there with irregular breaths of air that could hardly be called winds, and the whole of this day from midnight to midnight was all sunshine, contrasting marvelously with the dark icy storm-days we had experienced so short a time ago.

Herald Island came in sight at 1 o'clock p.m., and when we reached the edge of the pack, it was still about ten miles distant. We made our way through it, however, without great difficulty, as the ice was mostly light and had openings of clear water here and there, though in some close-packed fields the *Corwin* was pretty roughly bumped and had to steam her best to force a passage. At 10 o'clock p.m. we came to anchor in the midst of huge cakes and blocks about sixty-five feet thick, within two hundred or three hundred yards of the shore.

After so many futile efforts had been made to reach this little ice-bound island, everybody seemed wildly eager to run ashore and climb to the summit of its sheer granite cliffs. At first, a party of eight jumped from the bowsprit chains and ran across the narrow belt of margin ice and madly began to climb up an excessively steep gully, which came to an end in an inaccessible slope a few hundred feet above the water. Those ahead loosened and sent down a train of granite boulders, which shot over the heads of those below in a far more dangerous manner than any of the party seemed to appreciate. Fortunately nobody was hurt, and all made out to get down in safety. While this remarkable piece of mountaineering and Arctic exploration was in progress, a light skin-covered boat was dragged over the ice and launched on a strip of water that stretched in front of an accessible ravine, the bed of an ancient glacier, which I felt assured would conduct by an easy grade to the summit of the island. The slope of this ravine for the first one hundred feet or so was very steep, but inasmuch as it was full of firm, icy snow, it was easily ascended by cutting steps in the face of it with an ax that I had brought from the ship for the purpose. Beyond this there was not the slightest difficulty in our way, the glacier having graded a fine, broad road.

I first pushed on to the head of the glacier valley, and thence along the backbone of the island to the highest point, which I found to be about twelve hundred feet above the level of the sea. This point is about a mile and a half from the northwest end, and four and a half from the northeast end, thus making the island about six miles in length. It has been cut nearly in two by the glacial action it has undergone, the width at the lowest portion being about half a mile, and the average width about two miles. The entire island is a mass of granite, with the exception of a patch of metamorphic slate near the center. . . . This little island, standing as it does alone out in the Polar Sea, is a fine glacial monument.

The midnight hour I spent alone on the highest summit, one of the most impressive hours of my life. The deepest silence seemed to press down on all the vast, immeasurable virgin landscape. The sun near the horizon reddened the edges of belted cloud-bars, near the base of the sky, and the jagged ice boulders crowded together over the frozen ocean, stretching indefinitely northward, while more than a hundred miles of that mysterious Wrangell Land [Island] was seen blue, in the northwest, a wavering line of hill and dale over the white and blue ice-prairie, and pale gray mountains beyond, well calculated to fix the eye of a mountaineer, but it was to the far north that I ever found myself turning where the ice met the sky. I would fain have watched here all the strange night, but was compelled to remember the charge given me by the Captain to make haste and return to the ship as soon as I should find it possible, as there was ten miles of shifting, drifting ice between us and the open sea.

I therefore began the return journey about 1 o'clock this morning, after taking the compass bearings of the principal points within sight on

Wrangell Land [Island] and making a hasty collection of the flowering plants on my way.

Innumerable gulls and murres breed on the steep cliffs, the latter most abundant. They kept up a constant din of domestic notes. Some of them are sitting on their eggs, others have young, and it seems astonishing that either eggs or the young can find a resting place on cliffs so severely precipitous. The nurseries formed a living picture — the parents coming and going with food or to seek it, thousands in rows standing on narrow ledges like bottles on a grocer's shelves, the feeding of the little ones, the multitudes of wings, etc.

A fox was seen near the top of the northeast end of the island, and after we had all returned to the ship and were getting underway, the Captain discovered a polar bear swimming deliberately toward the ship between some floating blocks within a few yards of us.

Excerpt from John Muir, "The Jeannette Search. Exploration of Herald Island— No Signs of the Missing Ship. Dangers of Arctic Exploration—Fauna and Flora of the North. (Special Correspondence of the Bulletin.) Steamer Corwin (Off Herald Island), Arctic Ocean, July 31, 1881," *San Francisco Daily Evening Bulletin* (September 28, 1881): 4, col. 3.

FOUR MILE TRAIL

FROM 1882 UNTIL 1887, John Muir remained close to home, wrote few letters and fewer articles, and focused on the Strentzel-Muir ranch and practical horticulture. Louie could see that the ranch and profit were impairing her husband's health, and although she was no mountaineer, she proposed a visit to Yosemite, where perhaps Muir would be inspired. It was the Four-Mile Trail, built in 1871 by John Conway for James McCauley, that they climbed from Yosemite Valley to Glacier Point, to the small hotel constructed by McCauley and operated during the summer months. It would be Louie's first and last trip away from the Alhambra Valley. The Muirs, fearful of straying far from post or telegraph while in Yosemite, wrote to their daughter, (Annie) Wanda, who was staying with her grandparents, John and Louisiana Strentzel.

* * *

YOSEMITE VALLEY, JULY 16, 1884

My dear Wanda:

Papa & Mamma are coming home to baby tomorrow & Mamma & Papa have been glad all the time when Grandpa wrote a letter & baby wrote a letter that said "baby is well & good & does not cry at all." After Papa wrote the other letter to baby Mamma & Papa climbed up a high mountain & Mamma got tired & so Papa walked behind & pushed Mamma with a long stick this way & the stick soon began to hurt Mamma's back & then Mamma was too warm & so she took off some of her clothes & Papa tied a skirt on the end of the stick & then it did not hurt any more.

And when we were about half way up the mountain a man came up behind us with a horse & he said "How do you do, Mr. Muir" & I said "pretty well, this lady is Mrs. Muir, Mr. McCauley" & then he jumped down off his horse & said to Mamma "Please get on my horse Mrs. Muir" & there was a big mans saddle on the horse & some big bags that are called saddle bags & some meat & things in the bags but Mamma got on the top of it all & she looked very funny when she rode away up the mountain with the man behind with a stick whipping the horse to make him go fast.

And when we went to the top of the mountain we were hungry & the man gave us a good dinner & we looked off the top of the mountain & saw many beautiful waterfalls & trees & snow & rocks, & then we climbed up the side of another mountain & when we were climbing up Papa saw the marks of a bears foot & then Mamma was afraid but Papa said the bear is only looking for berries & will not bite. And then we told the man about the bear & the man said that an Indian saw the bear about half an hour before. And Mamma was afraid when she was picking flowers for the baby, & Papa has many stories to tell baby. And he & Mamma are coming home tomorrow.

"John Muir to Wanda Muir, Yosemite Valley, July 16, 1884," John Muir Papers, Holt-Atherton Department of Special Collections, University of the Pacific Library © 1984 Muir-Hanna Trust.

MOUNT RAINIER

I N SPRING 1887, JOHN MUIR was forty-nine when he accepted an offer from the J. Dewing Company to contribute to and edit *Picturesque California,* which included essays on Washington, Puget Sound, the Columbia River, and the Canadian Rockies. Sporadically he left the Strentzel-Muir ranch and took a room in a San Francisco hotel to concentrate on his writing, ultimately contributing six articles. Published in parts monthly, it was distributed to subscribers beginning in 1888 and continued through 1890. Preparation involved trips and on some of them Muir's friend, the landscape painter William Keith, accompanied him. The longest excursion began in July 1888 as far as Vancouver, but perhaps most arduous and memorable was the ascent on August 14 of Mount Rainier. Muir wrote to his wife that he had not intended to climb it, got excited, and soon found himself on the top. Joined by E. S. Ingraham, a relative of Jeanne Carr and superintendent of schools in Seattle; Philemon Beecher Van Trump, the postmaster at Yelm Prairie, a veteran mountaineer and their volunteer guide; and a group of five ambitious young climbers, they set out from Yelm Prairie, Washington, on the Tacoma and Oregon road, where they made their first camp.

* * *

JOURNAL ENTRY, AUGUST 9, 1888

We started at 10 a.m. with our huge, savage packs. A gypsy outfit would look tame and proper in comparison, what with our coffee-pot, capacity twenty quarts, alpenstocks, blankets, and grub—a ton.

We objected that the animals could not possibly endure the journey, and that our guide Joe was a mere boy, but were assured that the toughness of Washington mules was immeasurable, and that Joe was more than a man in woodcraft and knew the mysterious diamond hitch. With Van Trump as a volunteer we felt safe, but were determined to cut loose and walk to Rainier should the gypsy cavalcade fail by the way.

There was poison and sickness in every pot. The canned goods were at first called fresh, then in sickness were estimated to be ten years old, and at length, in agony of dyspepsia, their age was measured by centuries and antedated the forests primeval.

On we crawled mountainward, and with so noble a mark, undaunted, though drowsy and loitering, save when at intervals under the sharp spice of yellow jaundice, we all awoke to newness of life.

* * *

AN ASCENT OF MOUNT RAINIER, STEEP TRAILS

By night of the third day we reached the Soda Springs on the right bank of the Nisqually [River], which goes roaring by, gray with mud, gravel, and boulders from the caves of the glaciers of Rainier, now close at hand. The distance from the Soda Springs to the Camp of the Clouds is about ten miles. The first part of the way lies up the Nisqually Canyon, the bottom of which is flat in some places and the walls very high and precipitous, like those of the Yosemite Valley. The upper part of the canyon is still occupied by one of the Nisqually glaciers, from which this branch of the river draws its source, issuing from a cave in the gray, rock-strewn snout. About a mile below the glacier we had to ford the river, which caused some anxiety, for the current is very rapid and carried forward large boulders, as well as lighter material, while its savage roar is bewildering.

At this point we left the canyon, climbing out of it by a steep zigzag up the old lateral moraine of the glacier. . . . From the top of the moraine, still ascending, we passed for a mile or two through a forest of mixed growth . . . and then came to the charming park region, at an elevation of about five thousand feet above sea level. Here the vast, continuous woods at length begin to give way under the dominion of climate, though still at this height retaining their beauty and giving no sign of stress of storm, sweeping upward in belts of varying width . . . leaving smooth, spacious parks, with here and there separate groups of trees standing out in the midst of the openings like islands in a lake. Every one of these parks, great and small, is a garden filled knee-deep with fresh, lovely flowers of every hue, the most luxuriant and the most extravagantly beautiful of all the alpine gardens I ever beheld in all my mountain-top wanderings.

We arrived at the Cloud Camp at noon, but no clouds were in sight, save a few gauzy, ornamental wreaths adrift in the sunshine. Out of the forest at last, there stood the mountain, wholly unveiled, awful in bulk and majesty, filling all the view like a separate, newborn world, yet withal so fine and so beautiful it might well fire the dullest observer to desperate enthusiasm. Long we gazed in silent admiration, buried in tall daisies and anemones by the side of a snowbank. Higher we could not go with the animals and find food for them and wood for our own campfires, for just beyond this lies the region of ice, with only here and there an open spot on the ridges in the midst of the ice. . . . Here we lay all the afternoon, considering the lines of the mountains with reference to a way to the summit.

At noon next day we left camp and began our long climb. We were in light marching order, save one who pluckily determined to carry his camera to the summit. At night, after a long easy climb over wide and smooth fields of ice, we reached a narrow ridge, at an elevation of about ten thousand feet above the sea, on the divide between the glaciers of the Nisqually and the Cowlitz. Here we lay as best we could, waiting for another day, without fire of course, as we were now many miles beyond the timber-line and without much to cover us. After eating a little hardtack, each of us leveled a spot to lie on among lava-blocks and cinders. The night was cold, and the wind coming down upon us in stormy surges drove gritty ashes and fragments of pumice about our ears while chilling to the bone. Very short and shallow was our sleep that night; but day dawned at last, early rising was easy, and there was nothing about breakfast to cause any delay. About four o'clock we were off, and climbing began in earnest. We followed up the ridge on which we had spent the night, now along its crest, now on either side, or on the ice leaning against it, until we came to where it becomes massive and precipitous. Then we were compelled to crawl along a seam or narrow shelf on its face, which we traced to its termination in the base of the great ice-cap. From this point all the climbing was over ice, which was here desperately steep but fortunately was at the same time carved into innumerable spikes and pillars which afforded good footholds, and we crawled cautiously on, warm with ambition and exercise.

At length, after gaining the upper extreme of our guiding ridge, we found a good place to rest and prepare ourselves to scale the dangerous upper curves of the dome. The surface almost everywhere was bare, hard, snowless ice, extremely slippery; and, though smooth in general, it was interrupted by a network of yawning crevasses, outspread like lines of defense against any attempt to win the summit. Here every one of the party took off his shoes and drove stout steel caulks about half an inch long into them, having brought tools along for the purpose, and not having made use of them until now so that the points might not get dulled on the rocks ere the smooth, dangerous ice was reached. Besides being well-shod, each carried an alpenstock, and for special difficulties we had a hundred feet of rope and an axe.

Thus prepared, we stepped forth afresh, slowly groping our way through tangled lines of crevasses, crossing on snow bridges here and there after cautiously testing them, jumping at narrow places or crawling around the ends of the largest, bracing well at every point with our alpenstocks and setting our spiked shoes squarely down on the dangerous slopes. It was nerve-trying work, most of it, but we made good speed nevertheless, and by noon all stood together on the utmost summit, save one who, his strength failing for a time, came up later.

We remained on the summit nearly two hours, looking about us at the vast map-like views, comprehending hundreds of miles of the Cascade Range, with their black interminable forests and white volcanic cones in glorious array reaching far into Oregon, the Sound region also, and the great plains of eastern Washington, hazy and vague in the distance.

The descent was accomplished without disaster, though several of the party had narrow escapes. One slipped and fell, and as he shot past me seemed to be going to certain death. So steep was the ice-slope no one could move to help him, but fortunately, keeping his presence of mind, he threw himself on his face and digging his alpenstock into the ice, gradually retarded his motion until he came to rest. Another broke through a slim bridge over a crevasse, but his momentum at the time carried him against the lower edge and only his alpenstock was lost in the abyss. Thus crippled by the loss of his staff, we had to lower him the rest of the way down the dome by means of the rope we carried. Falling rocks from the upper precip-itous part of the ridge were also a source of danger, as they came whizzing past in successive volleys; but none told on us, and when we at length gained the gentle slopes of the lower ice-fields, we ran and slid at our ease, making fast, glad time, all care and danger past, and arrived at our beloved Cloud Camp before sundown.

We were rather weak from want of nourishment, and some suffered from sunburn, notwithstanding the partial protection of glasses and veils; otherwise, all were unscathed and well. The view we enjoyed from the sum-mit could hardly be surpassed in sublimity and grandeur; but one feels far from home so high in the sky, so much so that one is inclined to guess that, apart from the acquisition of knowledge and the exhilaration of climbing, more pleasure is to be found at the foot of mountains than on their frozen tops. Doubly happy, however, is the man to whom lofty mountaintops are within reach, for the lights that shine there illumine all that lies below.

Excerpt from Muir's journals in John Muir, *John of the Mountains: The Unpublished Journals of John Muir*, ed. Linnie Marsh Wolfe (Boston: Houghton Mifflin, 1938), 294. Excerpt from John Muir, *Steep Trails* (Boston: Houghton Mifflin, 1918), 263–70.

TUOLUMNE CANYON REVISITED

SINCE 1882, JOHN MUIR HAD BEEN busy managing the Strentzel-Muir ranch, caring for Louie's parents and their daughters, (Annie) Wanda, now eight, and Helen (Midge), born on January 23, 1886, now three. Editors and admirers had repeatedly asked Muir to begin writing again. Although he had taken on *Picturesque California* in the spring of 1887, it was not until the arrival in early June 1889, in San Francisco, of Robert Underwood Johnson, associate editor of *Century* magazine, that Muir found the encouragement he needed. His editorial mission included research on a series of articles on the gold rush and recruiting Muir to write for the magazine. Muir arranged a trip with Johnson to visit Yosemite Valley with a two-week pack trip into Tuolumne Meadows. They camped near Soda Springs, where discussions led to the launch of a campaign to create a national park around Yosemite Valley and the Mariposa Grove, currently managed by the State of California. Muir wrote two articles for *Century*, describing the region and outlining the boundaries for the proposed park—an appeal to the American people. Johnson, a persuasive lobbyist, presented the proposal in Washington, D.C., and New York. The bill, introduced in Congress in the fall of 1890, was passed on October 1, 1890. The dream of creating Yosemite National Park had been realized.

In 1892, due to Louie's efforts, Muir was relieved of the responsibility of managing the Strentzel-Muir ranch. His attention turned to the organization of the Sierra Club and the transfer of Yosemite Valley and the Mariposa Grove from California to the federal government and the new national park. A trip to Europe in 1893 included a visit to Muir's childhood home in Dunbar, Scotland, and he returned ready to prepare his first book. *The Mountains of California,* published in 1894 under Johnson's direction for the Century Company, was a collection of previously published selected articles.

A six-week ramble in August 1895 in Yosemite Valley and Yosemite National Park included Muir's return to the Tuolumne Canyon and the Hetch Hetchy Valley. Muir recorded the journey in a letter to his daughter (Annie) Wanda, in journal entries that begin on August 8 and conclude on August 13, and in a letter to his wife, Louie. Then fifty-seven, Muir progressed down the Tuolumne Canyon, discarding most of what he carried, arriving at Hetch Hetchy with only a handful of crackers and a pinch of tea. He set out to cover the twenty miles to Crocker's, a stopping place from 1880 until 1920 on the Big Oak Flat Road, about six miles northwest of the Tuolumne Grove. Muir hiked a few miles when he saw amateur photographer Theodore Parker Lukens on the trail. Lukens was a Pasadena banker, member of the Sierra Club, a published dendrologist, and a neighbor of Jeanne and Ezra S. Carr, who moved permanently to Pasadena in 1880.[1]

* * *

LETTER TO (ANNIE) WANDA MUIR

Monday, August 5, 1895

Dear Wanda:

I am just about to start afoot down the Tuolumne Canyon. Yesterday I climbed Mount Conness with two young men who joined me at Yosemite Valley and have been good bright manly company. It is about noon and here at the foot of the Big Tuolumne Meadows we part, they returning to Yosemite and I to go alone through the canyon to Hetch Hetchy and then to Crocker's and thence to Yosemite and home. I suppose I will be about two weeks in the canyon. I feel pretty well today after climbing and riding and crackers. My companions will lead back my horse, and I will be free in the wilderness again in the old way, without blankets, but I think I can stand it about as well as ever.

The flowers are lovely on the glacier meadows and on the high mountains, and you will never know how glad I am to be with them again. I am sitting on a rock by the river; and a cascade is chanting gloriously, and all the old enthusiasm has come again.

I will have a hard grand trip and will be cold a little at night but will not suffer, for I know well how to use a campfire. I wrote to Helen before leaving Yosemite and will write your mother when I return. Love to all. How gloriously the river is singing. Ever affectionately your father.

John Muir

* * *

JOURNAL ENTRIES, 1895

Camp at the head of Muir Gorge, Tuolumne Canyon, August 8

I saw two rattlesnakes today, neither of which threatened me. One was of a species new to me; I did not at first take it for a rattler. It was rather slender, beautifully colored, black and white in triangular pattern. The other was a common dull-gray fellow, thick and muscular that I came upon suddenly. Towards night in pushing through brush and rocks, I threw my bundle ahead of me. It fell plump on the rattler. He, highly indignant, crawled away a few feet and coiled and thundered. I cautiously withdrew my bundle and passed him a few feet away, he eyeing me suspiciously in wonder and striking at me. It was a rough place; but it was getting late, and I was then at the head of the Muir Gorge and had to camp. I decided to camp on top of a large boulder a snake could not climb except by a log that leaned against it. This I managed to remove. The boulder was about twelve by fifteen feet, sloping like a house roof, but a slight hollow in the middle enabled me to keep from falling. I built a row of stones that barely would lie, for bed and fire, and here I cooked and even slept hard, waking only four times to tend the fire.

Camp in Hetch Hetchy, August 13

Left camp at 6:30 a.m. to go to Crocker's. On the trail I met Mr. T. P. Lukens of Pasadena with a complete outfit. I told him I had intended remaining longer in the valley but was driven out by want of food, having been compelled to throw away most of what I started down the canyon with. He said he had abundance and proposed my returning to the valley for a few days. This I was quite willing to do.

We camped about the middle of Hetch Hetchy and soon had a portable table set and covered with new dishes of every description, and had bacon, potatoes, tomatoes, and bread. I felt hungry only after I had eaten well. Potatoes seemed especially good to me. I had only a handful of crackers left and tea when found, which I emptied by the side of the trail. Left my cup also. My outfit was a contrast to Mr. Lukens's.

* * *

LETTER TO LOUIE WANDA STRENTZEL MUIR

Crocker's Station, August 17 or 18, 1895

Dear Louie:

I reached this cool calm nest in the sugar pines last evening. I think you will remember the place. It is not far from the Tuolumne sequoia grove where we had lunch on the way to the valley 10 years ago.

I sent a pencil note to Wanda from the Tuolumne Meadows at the head of the great canyon by Mr. Howard, which I suppose was received. I had taken two of the Howard boys (Spring Valley Howards) to the top of

Conness and left them at the Meadows; they to return to Yosemite, and I to go down the Canyon to Hetch Hetchy where I had ordered horses to meet me about the 20th. Well, I had a hard time and a good time, and anyhow by this, you see I got through safely. I started with provisions for three weeks; but after breaking my way for a few miles through the rocks and brush, I found it was too heavy and bulky and so had to throw half of it away. . . . I couldn't eat much, only a handful of crackers and bite of chocolate, no matter how hard I scrambled, so I threw away half of what was left when I was about [in] the middle of the canyon, for the weather was hot during the day, and I soon was very tired. I carried that extra thick suit of underclothing to draw on at night as I had no blanket, but I abandoned that also and then got on better, though of course cold at night. . . . I couldn't eat and was of course growing very thin and gaunt, but nevertheless I climbed and made my way with the old skill and the old love and was very far from fainting by the way. I sketched and made the notes I wanted, took my time, and in spite of all disadvantages greatly enjoyed the glorious river in its glorious home.

When at length I reached Hetch Hetchy, I had only two handfuls of little square crackers and tea. I bathed and washed my underclothes, stayed a day sketching, writing, etc. . . . I having no food, had to set out for Crocker's, twenty miles on foot. This seemed only a comfortable saunter, weak though I was after the canyon work. But now came a change. After I had climbed out of Hetch Hetchy two or three miles on my way to Crocker's, I met a big good-natured dog on the trail, then a big good-natured man on horseback, then another man came in sight around a bend in the trail, and two laden pack animals, etc. The gentleman in the lead asked me my name, then told me he had come to meet me and came so early to make sure of not missing me or keeping me waiting. He, Mr. Lukens, is a banker stopping at Crocker's for his health, said he was glad of the chance of knowing John Muir, and so organized this expedition at his own expense and refused to allow me to pay for anything. Well, he offered to open a pack and feed me when we met on the trail, but I was not hungry. We returned to Hetch Hetchy and camped there on the bank of the beautiful river beneath a Kellogg Oak, and remained three days making photos of the scenery, fishing for trout, eating, etc. I left my handful of crackers by the roadside, and when I sat down to the bountiful table of Mr. Lukens, my appetite came back, and I have been eating ever since.

Excerpt from "John Muir to Wanda Muir, August 5, 1895," John Muir Papers, University of the Muir Papers, University of the Pacific © 1984 Muir–Hanna Trust. Excerpt from Muir's journals in John Muir, *John of the Mountains: The Unpublished Journals of John Muir*, ed. Linnie Marsh Wolfe (Boston: Houghton Mifflin, 1938), 344–45; 347. Excerpt from "John Muir to Louie Strentzel Muir, Crocker's Station, August 17 or 18, 1895," John Muir Papers, Holt-Atherton Department of Special Collections, University of the Pacific Library © 1984 Muir–Hanna Trust.

THE MONKEY PUZZLE TREES

W HEN JOHN MUIR TRAVELED through the southern United States in 1867 on his thousand-mile
walk to the Gulf of Mexico, he intended to continue on to
South America, following in the footsteps of Alexander von
Humboldt, who traced the course of the Orinoco River,
explored the Amazon, and returned to Europe with over
sixty thousand plant specimens. Still weak with malaria, the
respite Muir sought in Havana did little to restore his health
and that, combined with his inability to find a ship bound for
South America, resulted in his ultimately traveling north to
New York and west to California. Muir's plan was to remain
in California for a year, then resume his quest to reach the
Amazon.[1]

It was more than forty years before Muir achieved this
goal, and it was a trip that lasted eight months and covered
forty thousand miles from South America to Africa. Departing from Brooklyn, New York, on August 12, 1911, at the age
of seventy-three, Muir sailed in search of indigenous trees.
The real prize was the rare *Araucaria imbricata*, known as the

monkey puzzle tree, because its prickly needles render it impossible for monkeys to reach the fruit that grows at the very top.[2]

Traveling by train from Buenos Aires, Argentina, to Santiago, Chile, Muir visited the Santiago Botanical Gardens, where he researched the elevation, temperature, and soil conditions in which the monkey puzzle trees grow. He traveled an additional five hundred miles south to Victoria, Chile, and proceeded by horse and buggy and then on horseback with an excursion party into the mountains. Near the snowline on the western slope of the Andes on November 20, Muir spotted the trees growing along a ridge high above a glacier meadow. He sketched the trees in his journal, spent the night in the aboriginal forest, and descended the next day.[3]

* * *

JOURNAL ENTRIES, 1911

November 20.

Foggy morning. At 6:00 a.m. packing for the lofty ridges where grows *Araucaria imbricata*. Last evening rode over to John Hunter's, who has a sawmill. Kindly gave up work to guide us to the forests I've so long wished to see. Hard but glorious day. Camped before sunset. Rode through magnificent forest of round-headed trees, some of them evergreens. Where soil is well-watered the average height of the principal trees must exceed a hundred feet. Some nearly 150 feet high. Our party consists of Mr. Smith,

Mr. Williams, Mr. Hunter, myself, two Chilean packers, all well-mounted, well-clad, and provisioned. After crossing many hilly ridges and streams, ferny and mossy and spacious meadows, came in full sight of a ridge one thousand feet high bordering the south side of a glacier meadow, the top of which was fringed with the long-sought-for *Araucaria*. Long scramble up the steep grassy slope and brush. One horse fell and rolled. Traced the ridge a mile or two, admiring; then descended long cane-covered S. slope to the bottom of another glacier meadow valley by the side of a brawling bouldery stream and encamped beneath an *Araucaria* grove. *Araucaria* in scattered groups or singly all way down and up S. slope and fringing the horizon all around. A glorious and novel sight, beyond all I had hoped for. Yet I had so long dreamed of it, it seemed familiar. My three companions slept under tarpaulin tents, strangely fearing the blessed mountain air and dew.

The bark of the trees varies very much in thickness and pattern. On some it is smooth; on others deeply cut into squares or rhombs like alligator skin, from half an inch to nearly two inches in diameter.

November 21.

Traced the South ridge above our camp, sketching and photographing six views of the ancient forest. Obtained a male and female flower and cones and started on the return trip to the Smith ranch, by a way several miles to the southward of the way we came up, thus obtaining new views of the magnificent, round-headed forest trees extending over the whole plateau as far as the eye could reach, and interrupted only by small grassy prairies and meadows. I think it is without exception the tallest forest of round-headed trees that I have ever seen, averaging mile after mile over a hundred feet in height. Many beautiful trees and shrubs were in flower, especially around the meadow and prairie openings. One shrub in particular, usually eight to ten feet in height, was covered with brilliant scarlet flowers, making a magnificent border to the forest. Many of the trees, too, had their trunks and larger branches adorned with ferns of many species and beautiful parasites and epiphytes.

Arrived at the Smith ranch in the evening of the same day as left the *Araucaria* woods. We noted in several places a lone *Araucaria* growing in the beech and laurel groves, especially on the edges of the groves, six or eight miles from the lower edge of the main *Araucaria* belt.

Excerpts from "John Muir, November 1911–March 1912, Trip to South America, Part III, and Trip to Africa Journal," 25–26, John Muir Papers, Holt-Atherton Department of Special Collections, University of the Pacific Library © 1984 Muir-Hanna Trust.

EPILOGUE

John Muir's purpose had always been to study the natural world until he was too old to climb mountains. But in his midsixties he realized that he needed to prepare his notes, journals, and articles that had not already been published in his first two books: *The Mountains of California* (1894) and *Our National Parks* (1901). There would be a forward push to accomplish this goal in spite of events that hampered his progress. Muir and President Theodore Roosevelt spent three nights camped in Yosemite in 1903, during which Muir talked about the need for California to recede Yosemite Valley and the Mariposa Grove to the federal government. Returning to the Alhambra Valley, Muir immediately departed for the East Coast and sailed to Europe for a world tour, traveling at first with Charles S. Sargent, the director of Harvard University's Arnold Arboretum in Boston, Massachusetts, and Sargent's son Robeson.

On May 27, 1904, Muir returned to the United States, to the dock in San Francisco, where his daughters Wanda and Helen stood waiting. At the ranch Louie welcomed him home. Louie died in 1905, and to Muir, the Alhambra Valley house no longer felt like home. The days and nights he spent with Roosevelt in 1903 did have a lasting effect, with the passage of a bill on June 11, 1906, receding Yosemite Valley and the Mariposa Grove to become part of the surrounding Yosemite National Park. The death of Muir's close friends, William Keith (in 1911) and John Swett (in 1913), contributed to his lingering sadness. That sorrow only grew with the passage of the Raker bill, which transferred the Hetch Hetchy Valley from Yosemite National Park to San Francisco for use as a reservoir. Soon Yosemite Valley's twin would be buried under tons of water with the building of the O'Shaughnessy Dam.[1]

John Muir passed away from pneumonia on December 24, 1914, in the California Hospital in Los Angeles. At the time he was visiting his daughter Helen and her family in Daggett, California, near Barstow, having taken the train from the Alhambra Valley to celebrate Christmas. His life well spent. His journeys never long enough. Farewell.

NOTES

INTRODUCTION

1. John Muir, *A Thousand Mile Walk to the Gulf* (Boston: Houghton Mifflin, 1916), 139.

2. "John Muir to Mrs. Ezra S. Carr, Trout's Mills, near Meaford, September 13, [1865]," in John Muir, *Letters to a Friend: Written to Mrs. Ezra S. Carr, 1866–1879* (Boston: Houghton Mifflin, 1915), 8–15.

3. "John Muir to Mrs. Ezra S. Carr, Yosemite Valley, October 7, 1874," in ibid., 168–69.

4. Samuel Hall Young, *Alaska Days with John Muir* (New York: Fleming H. Revell, 1915), 627–28. "John Muir to Jeanne C. Carr, Indianapolis, August 30, 1867," in Muir, *Letters to a Friend,* 31–32.

CALYPSO BOREALIS

1. The *Calypso borealis* is known today as the *Calypso bulbosa.* The common name is "lady slipper orchid" or "hider of the north" as it favors sheltered areas. Growing in bogs or wet woods, its single small pink, purple, or magenta flower is accented with a white lip, darker-purple spotting, and a yellow beard. Though not indentical to the *Calypso bulbosa var. americana* Muir found in Canada, the *Calypso bulbosa var. occidentalis* orchid is found in the Sierra Nevada. The range of *Calypso* orchids is circumboreal and includes most of the northerly states of the United States and Canada.

BONAVENTURE CEMETERY

1. William Frederic Badè, *The Life and Letters of John Muir*, vol. 1 (Boston: Houghton Mifflin, 1924), 156.

2. Muir refers to "unhealthy vapors" during his stay in the Bonaventure Cemetery. He assumed that a miasma (bad air)—usually night air, rising from putrefying vegetation—caused the malaria from which he suffered. In 1880 scientists discovered a group of parasitic protozoans known as Plasmodium. In 1900 these protozoans were identified as the cause of malaria, contracted from the bite of a mosquito. Muir was most likely bitten while in the Bonaventure Cemetery.

FIRST TRIP TO YOSEMITE

1. "John Muir to David Gilrye Muir, Cedar Keys, Florida, December 13, 1867," John Muir Papers, Holt-Atherton Department of Special Collections, University of the Pacific Library © 1984 Muir-Hanna Trust.

2. Galen Clark arrived in Yosemite Valley in August 1855. On March 19, 1856, he filed a claim on 160 acres along the Merced River South Fork. In April 1857 he built a log cabin, known as Clark's Station. At the end of 1874, the property was sold to Henry, John, and Edward Washburn, who further developed Clark's wayside inn. Completed in the spring of 1879, Clark's Station was renamed the Wawona Hotel in 1882.

SEQUOIA INK

1. "Duchess" is a reference to Thérèse Yelverton, Viscountess Avonmore.

EMERSON, KEEP YOUR NOSE OUT OF DOORS

1. Muir's name was the last to appear on a short list Emerson kept titled "My Men." Muir believed that Emerson was the most sequoia-like soul he had ever met.

CHRISTMAS SHEEP

1. "John Muir to Mrs. Ezra S. Carr, Yosemite, August 13, [1871]," in Muir, *Letters to a Friend*, 102–4. "John Muir to Ann Gilrye Muir, Yosemite Valley, November 16, 1871," John Muir Papers, Holt-Atherton Department of Special Collections, University of the Pacific Library © 1984 Muir-Hanna Trust.

FIRST EXPLORATION OF THE SOUTHERN SIERRA

1. "John Muir to Mrs. Ezra S. Carr, Yosemite Valley, June 7, 1873," in Muir, *Letters to a Friend*, 154.

2. "John Muir to Sarah Muir Galloway, Yosemite Valley, September 3, 1873," John Muir Papers, Holt-Atherton Department of Special Collections, University of the Pacific Library © 1984 Muir-Hanna Trust.

3. John Muir's reference to Mount Tyndall may actually have been Mount Brewer or a peak on the Kings–Kern divide.

A SHASTA STORM

1. "John Muir to Mrs. Ezra S. Carr, Yosemite Valley, October 7, 1874," in Muir, *Letters to a Friend*, 168–69.

2. "John Muir to Mrs. Ezra S. Carr, Sisson's Station, November 1, 1874," in ibid., 170–72.

SHASTA BEES

1. John Muir, "A Wind Storm in the Forests of the Yuba," *Scribner's Monthly* 17 (November 1878): 59.

2. "John Muir to Sarah Galloway Muir, Oakland, [California], January 16, 1875," John Muir Papers, Holt-Atherton Department of Special Collections, University of the Pacific Library © 1984 Muir-Hanna Trust.

HALF DOME

1. John Muir, "South Dome, Its Ascent by George Anderson and John Muir— Hard Climbing but a Glorious View—Botany of the Dome—Yosemite in Late Autumn. (From Our Own Special Correspondent.) Yosemite Valley, November 10, 1875," *San Francisco Daily Evening Bulletin* (November 18, 1875): 1, col. 1. John Muir, "Summering in the Sierra. The Summit of South Dome—Yosemite Tourists—An Irrepressible Mountain Climber. (From Our Own Correspondent.) Yosemite Valley, August 28, 1876," *San Francisco Daily Evening Bulletin* (September 6, 1876): 1, col. 4.

WATER OUZEL

1. John Muir, "Wild Parks and Forest Reservations of the West," *Atlantic Monthly* 81 (January 1898): 21.

TAHOE IN WINTER

1. "John Muir to Annie Kennedy Bidwell, 1419 Taylor Street, San Francisco, March 28, 1878," John Muir Papers, Holt-Atherton Department of Special Collections, University of the Pacific Library © 1984 Muir-Hanna Trust.

HERALD ISLAND

1. "John Muir to Louie Wanda Strentzel, San Francisco, April 18, 1879," John Muir Papers, Holt-Atherton Department of Special Collections, University of the Pacific Library © 1984 Muir-Hanna Trust.

TUOLUMNE CANYON REVISITED

1. After five days at Crocker's, Muir joined a party and set out again for Tuolumne Meadows, climbing to the top of Mount Conness. Through a snowstorm he returned to Tuolumne Meadows. He had never seen snow in the meadows in August. After several days in Yosemite Valley, he stopped at Wawona to see the sequoia grove, then headed home to Martinez, California.

THE MONKEY PUZZLE TREES

1. John Muir, *A Thousand-Mile Walk to the Gulf*, 169–70. "John Muir to Mrs. Ezra S. Carr, Tuolumne River, two miles below La Grange, November 4, [1870]," in Muir, *Letters to a Friend*, 93–96.

2. John Muir, *John Muir's Last Journey. South to the Amazon and East to Africa. Unpublished Journals and Selected Correspondence*, ed. Michael P. Branch (Washington, D.C.: Island Press, 2001), xxxiii–xxxiv, xxxix.

3. Linnie Marsh Wolfe, *Son of the Wilderness: The Life of John Muir* (New York: Alfred A. Knopf, 1945), 332. Muir stayed at the Smith ranch in Victoria, Chile. Smith was a local logger. Muir, *John Muir's Last Journey*, 104–5.

EPILOGUE

1. John Muir published the following books: *The Mountains of California* (1894), *Our National Parks* (1901), *Stickeen* (1909), *My First Summer in the Sierra* (1911), *The Yosemite* (1912), and *The Story of My Boyhood and Youth* (1913). The following books were published posthumously: *Travels in Alaska* (1915), *A Thousand-Mile Walk to the Gulf* (1916), *The Cruise of the Corwin* (1917), and *Steep Trails* (1918). Wolfe, *Son of the Wilderness*, 301.

BIBLIOGRAPHY

Badè, William Frederic, ed. *The Life and Letters of John Muir*. 2 vols. Boston: Houghton Mifflin, 1924.

"For the Boston Recorder. The Calypso Borealis. Botanical Enthusiasm. From Prof. J. D. Butler." *Boston Recorder* (December 21, 1866): 1.

John Muir Papers. Holt-Atherton Department of Special Collections. University of the Pacific Library © 1984 Muir-Hanna Trust.

Johnson, Robert Underwood. *Remembered Yesterdays*. Boston: Little, Brown, and Company, 1923.

Muir, John. "Explorations in the Great Tuolumne Cañon." *Overland Monthly* 11 (August 1873): 139–47.

———. "South Dome, Its Ascent by George Anderson and John Muir—Hard Climbing but a Glorious View—Botany of the Dome—Yosemite in Late Autumn. (From Our Own Special Correspondent.) Yosemite Valley, November 10, 1875." *San Francisco Daily Evening Bulletin* (November 18, 1875): 1, col. 1.

———. "The Humming-Bird of the California Water-Falls." *Scribner's Monthly* 15 (February 1878): 545–54.

———. "In the Yo-Semite: Holidays Among the Rocks. Wild Weather— A Picturesque Christmas Dinner—Idyllic Amusements—Poetic Storms—

A Paradise of Clouds. Yo-semite Valley, January 1." *New York Weekly Tribune* (March 13, 1872): 3, cols. 4–5.

———. "The Jeannette Search: Exploration of Herald Island—No Signs of the Missing Ship. Dangers of Arctic Exploration—Fauna and Flora of the North. (Special Correspondence of the Bulletin.) Steamer Corwin (Off Herald Island), Arctic Ocean, July 31, 1881." *San Francisco Daily Evening Bulletin* (September 28, 1881): 4, col. 3.

———. *John Muir's Last Journey: South to the Amazon and East to Africa. Unpublished Journals and Selected Correspondence.* Edited by Michael P. Branch. Washington, D.C.: Island Press, 2001.

———. *John of the Mountains: The Unpublished Journals of John Muir.* Edited by Linnie Marsh Wolfe. Boston: Houghton Mifflin, 1938.

———. *Letters to a Friend: Written to Mrs. Ezra S. Carr, 1866–1879.* Boston: Houghton Mifflin, 1915.

———. "Living Glaciers of California." *Harper's New Monthly Magazine* 51 (November 1875): 769–76.

———. "Mount Whitney. Its Ascent by John Muir, the Explorer and Geologist. Different Routes—The Ascent from the East—A Minor Yosemite—Glacier Meadows and Glacier Lakes—Glorious Views—Successive Ascents. (Special Correspondence of the Bulletin.) Independence, Inyo County, August 17, 1875." *San Francisco Daily Evening Bulletin* (August 24, 1875): 1, cols. 2–3.

———. "Notes From Utah. John Muir the Naturalist, on Bathing in Salt Lake—A Glorious Swim—Erroneous Impressions Corrected. (Special Correspondent of the Bulletin.) Lake Point, Utah, May 20, 1877." *San Francisco Daily Evening Bulletin* (June 14, 1877): 1, col. 1.

———. "Rambles of a Botanist Among the Plants and Climates of California." *Old and New* 5 (June 1872): 767–72.

———. "Shasta Bees. A Honeyful Region—The Bee Lands—A Summer Paradise. (From Our Special Correspondent.) Sisson's Station near Mt. Shasta, December 17, 1874." *San Francisco Daily Evening Bulletin* (January 5, 1875): 2, col. 5.

———. "Shasta in Winter. John Muir, the Geologist and Explorer, Ascends It. A Hard and Perilous Undertaking—Among the Glaciers, Lava-beds, and Storm-clouds. (Special Correspondence of the Bulletin.) Sisson's Station, November 24, 1874." *San Francisco Daily Evening Bulletin* (December 2, 1874): 1, col. 3.

———. "South Dome, Its Ascent by George Anderson and John Muir—Hard Climbing but a Glorious View—Botany of the Dome—Yosemite in Late Autumn. (From Our Special Correspondent.) Yosemite Valley, November 10, 1875." *San Francisco Daily Evening Bulletin* (November 18, 1875): 1, col. 1.

———. *Steep Trails.* Boston: Houghton Mifflin, 1918.

———. "Summering in the Sierra. The Summit of South Dome—Yosemite Tourists—An Irrepressible Mountain Climber. (From Our Own Correspondent.) Yosemite Valley, August 28, 1876." *San Francisco Daily Evening Bulletin* (September 6, 1876): 1, col. 4.

———. "Tahoe in Winter. John Muir Gives Some Curious Facts About Sierra Snow—Stored Up Snow Masses—Glacial Lakes—Snow Shoe Experiences—A Retired Hunter. (Correspondence of the Bulletin)." *San Francisco Daily Evening Bulletin* (April 3, 1878): 4, cols. 1–2.

———. "A Talk by John Muir After a Dinner Given to Him and Certain Members of the American Alpine Club by Judge Harrington Putnam at the Manhattan Hotel, New York, June 17, 1911, From Notes By Alden Sampson." *Sierra Club Bulletin* 12 (January 1924): 43–46.

———. *A Thousand-Mile Walk to the Gulf.* Boston: Houghton Mifflin, 1916.

————. "Wild Parks and Forest Reservations of the West." *Atlantic Monthly* 81 (January 1898): 15–28.

————. "Wild Wool." *Overland Monthly* 14 (April 1875): 361–66.

————. "A Wind Storm in the Forests of the Yuba." *Scribner's Monthly* 17 (November 1878): 55–59.

Wolfe, Linnie Marsh. *Son of the Wilderness: The Life of John Muir.* New York: Alfred A. Knopf, 1945.

Young, Samuel Hall. *Alaska Days with John Muir.* New York: Fleming H. Revell, 1915.

ABOUT THE EDITOR

BONNIE J. GISEL is an environmental historian, the author of *Nature's Beloved Son: Rediscovering John Muir's Botanical Legacy* (Heyday Books, 2008), and the editor of *Kindred and Related Spirits: The Letters of John Muir and Jeanne C. Carr* (University of Utah Press, 2001). Having published articles and lectured extensively on John Muir, Gisel curated the traveling exhibit based on *Nature's Beloved Son* for Exhibit Envoy (2011–15). She also served as a consultant on the exhibit *A Walk in the Wild: Continuing John Muir's Journey*, for the Oakland Museum of California (2008–11). She co-chaired the 2010 conference "John Muir and Science" at the University of the Pacific and chaired the 2001 conference "John Muir: Family and Friends," also held at the University of the Pacific. Gisel has taught environmental history at the University of the Pacific (where she was interim director of the John Muir Center for Environmental Studies from 2000 to 2001), the Caspersen School of Graduate Studies at Drew University (where she received a PhD), and Green Mountain College.

ABOUT THE ARTIST

FIONA KING attended the Kootenay School of the Arts in Nelson, British Columbia. For more than thirty years she has focused exclusively on product, editorial, publishing, and corporate illustration assignments. Fiona has illustrated many books, including the award-winning *The Wild Muir: Twenty-two of John Muir's Greatest Adventures*, edited by Lee Stetson (Yosemite Conservancy, 1994), and the People of the Book series. More than twenty of her illustrations are installed at the new Old Faithful Visitor Education Center at Yellowstone National Park. Fiona moved to southwestern Colorado in 2003 and built a passive solar house in McElmo Canyon. When not at her drawing board, she spends as much time as possible hiking and backpacking through the beautiful red rock canyons and forested mountains of the Four Corners area. Visit fionart.com.

CREDITS